MARTIN LUTHER REFORMER IN THE MAKING

Erwin R. Scharf

NORTHWESTERN PUBLISHING HOUSE
Milwaukee, Wisconsin

Cover Design and Page Layout by Matthew P. Schaser
Illustrated by Harold Schmitz and Harold Paulsen

Library of Congress Card 87-61220

Northwestern Publishing House
1250 N. 113th St., P.O. Box 26975, Milwaukee, WI 53226-0975
© 1987 by Northwestern Publishing House.
Published 1987
Printed in the United States of America
ISBN 0-8100-0268-X

CONTENTS

FOREWORD

I am delighted and grateful to have been privileged to be an early reader of Professor Scharf's engaging lectures on the life and work of the great Reformer. They should make rewarding reading for Lutheran (and other) clergy and laity. They should be particularly so for those who have not had, or have not now, the opportunity of direct access to Luther's own powerful and influential writings themselves. It is my earnest hope that both clergy and laity will proceed to become regular readers of the incomparable legacy Luther has left the church.

I congratulate my good friend and leading member of my own Northwestern College Class of 1928 upon writing so informative and empathetic a book destined to lead to a more intimate acquaintance with the genius of the Reformation. Graduates of Northwestern who took his splendid course on the Reformation can now renew part of the experience. Others who may not have had Professor Scharf in class or who have not heard him deliver these lectures in person, will now be able to peruse them in the quiet of their homes.

The reason why I am including a reference to the clergy in my prefatory lines is that I trust they may now be more induced than ever to open some of the pages of the great Weimar edition of Luther's works, the most impressive and most scholarly edition accorded any human author. The finest Luther scholars in the world are deeply troubled by the still increasing ignorance of Luther (*Luthervergessenheit*). They plead for real and personal involvement with the greatest figure in the history of Christianity since St. Paul himself.

Remember: Dr. Ott bought the *Weimarana* for the Northwestern Library, and Professor Scharf helped catalogue it I am sure. A Northwestern graduate should not have to settle for English translations of Luther's works. What better use can we make of the many years of Latin and German we had in Watertown.

I am confident the late Martin Franzmann, Lenore Geweke, Gerhard Redlin, Heinrich Vogel and the others are joining us in spirit to offer congratulations to our classmate Erwin Scharf on this happy occasion.

The Newberry Library
June 28, 1987   Heinz Bluhm '28

PREFACE

It was early in 1982, the year before the quincentenary anniversary of the birthday of Martin Luther, when a committee of the faculty at Wisconsin Lutheran Seminary in Mequon, Wisconsin, asked the undersigned to prepare a series of essays for the five Monday afternoon sessions of the 1983 Fall Pastors' Institute. The Institute was to be held at the Seminary in Mequon.

It was the wish of that committee that these essays should concern themselves with the theme, "Martin Luther, the Reformer in the Making."

Although through the years a multitude of Luther biographies have found their way onto library shelves all over the world, the committee was of the opinion that this particular theme had not been too fully or too frequently treated by English-speaking authors.

After the five essays had been read in Mequon, invitations were received to read them in five other districts of the Wisconsin Synod. More recently it was suggested that the material be published in the form of a book.

Those who read these pages will realize that they were not meant to provide an exhaustive biography of Luther or history of the Reformation. It is the author's wish, however, that the reader will find this account worthwhile and helpful to his understanding of the way in which God guided the young Luther along a difficult and challenging pathway to the threshold of the Reformation.

Finally, the undersigned wishes to extend his genuine gratitude to the Rev. John A. Trapp, a member of the editorial staff of the Northwestern Publishing House, for offering his kind encouragement and for serving as editor of this little volume.

Watertown, Wisconsin
June, 1987

Erwin R. Scharf

CHAPTER ONE

BACKGROUND AND CHILDHOOD

It has been said that the times make the man. There is much evidence in favor of applying that cliché to Martin Luther, the Reformer, and his times. Yet in Luther's case the evidence prefers the conclusion that God makes both the times and the man.

It is always a thrilling experience for a Christian student of history to be able to trace the movement of the Lord's guiding hand as it prepared the way for some great event in history. These occasions are not always as clear as when God readied the world for the birth of the Savior, so that an inspired Paul could speak of it as "the fullness of time." But the times immediately preceding the birth of Luther, the cultural awakening called the Renaissance, providentially prepared the world for Luther and the Lutheran Reformation. The light at the end of the Dark Ages signaled the revival of learning, the study of the classical languages, the development of the fine arts, improvement in transportation, the discovery of new worlds and a long list of inventions, among them the printing press. Humanly speaking, it is difficult to imagine how Luther could have become the reformer that he was, or how his reformation could have had a lasting, world-wide influence without the Renaissance.

Another prime factor was the condition of the church of that day and the situation into which the papacy had gotten itself by this time. Many historians agree that it had fallen to its all-time low. The Renaissance popes were a despicably sorry lot. It is hard to understand how they could think of themselves as members of the Christian clergy, not to mention the head of the church. It is equally hard to understand how the people of that age put up with them in that role, except for the fact that they did so in ignorance and out of a superstitious clinging to their traditions. What did Luther hear as a boy at the supper table, and what rumors drifted up from Rome to Erfurt and Wittenberg while the Reformer was in the making? There was Alexander VI, a member of the wealthy Borgia family in Spain. His reign as pope was marred by adultery, deception and murder. Alexander supported the machinations of his depraved son, Caesar Borgia, whom Machiavelli used as the unscrupulous model for his book, *The Prince*. Alexander's daughter, Lucretia, was an acme of immorality. All in all, from the standpoint of public morality, he brought the papacy to the bottom. Luther was a young lad of nine when Alexander started ruling and was already a student at the University of Erfurt by the end of his reign.

The next pope, Julius II, gave the church of his day little to celebrate about. History calls him the "warrior pope" and his reign the "pontificate terrible." He tried to impress his constituents by marching his armies through the streets of Rome. The League of

Cambrai and the Holy League attest to his international maneuvering in the interest of increasing his secular power. The great humanist, perhaps also humorist, Erasmus, saw Julius on one occasion marching his army through the streets of Rome. Later he wrote a play in his usual satirical style in which he pictured Peter as rejecting Julius at the gate of heaven. Erasmus was trying to show how much the papacy had deteriorated between the reigns of Peter and Julius. He pictured them as two popes who could not understand each other. When Peter told Julius that he would need faith to enter Paradise, Julius pleaded that he had never heard of faith. And when Julius threatened to excommunicate Peter, the latter said that he was unable to understand what he meant since excommunication was not known in his day as pope. Julius was still pope when Luther visited Rome as a young monk in 1510, but the two did not meet. Julius was out of town on a military adventure.

The next Renaissance pope, Leo X, was a member of the wealthy Medici family of Florence, a son of Lorenzo the Magnificent. Spoiled completely by his wastefully wealthy background, Leo was determined to complete and to exceed the plans of Julius for a new Vatican and St. Peter's Cathedral. Having squandered his own share of the family fortune at the races and on women, as one historian puts it, Julius had to rely on his income from the sale of indulgences. Luther responded to the practice in 1517, and his hammer blows were felt in Rome.

There is one other event which was to play a significant role in discrediting the papacy at the time of the

Reformation. About 40 years before the birth of Luther, Laurentius Valla, the Renaissance scholar from Spain, revealed the spuriousness of a document known as the *Donation of Constantine*. This document was a forgery which held the gullible, medieval mind under the thumb of the papacy during the Dark Ages. It did have a predecessor, they believed, in the form of another document, the *Donation of Pippin*. The first Frankish Carolingian ruler, Pippin the Short, answered a call for help from Stephen II, the Bishop of Rome, against the troublesome Lombards in northern Italy. After Pippin had conquered the Lombards, he realized that he could hardly hope to rule them adequately all the way from Germany, north of the Alps. For that reason he turned over what became the Papal States to the Bishop of Rome. That was a genuine donation. Charlemagne later renewed it, as did also Otto the Great.

After about five centuries, however, it happened that the Roman Catholic Church of the West was in danger of falling apart into a welter of tribal, royal or feudal churches. In that day of confusion a document appeared, known as the *Donation of Constantine*. It claimed that Constantine, way back in the early fourth century, had showed his gratitude to the Bishop of Rome for healing him from leprosy by issuing the *Donation* to the Bishop and the Bishop's successors. It purportedly offered as a gift, or donation, the city of Rome and all the provinces, districts and cities of Italy — in other words, all of the territory that made up western Europe, the western half of the empire which Constantine had ruled.

Because of this document the gullible folk of the Dark Ages yielded their rights to the Bishop of Rome for about eight centuries. It was, of course, a cleverly contrived document. Its structure was similar to that of the real *Donation of Pippin* and sounded a little like another decree which Constantine actually did issue when he moved his capital from Rome to Constantinople. That document allowed the Bishop of Rome to use state authority in the West to enforce doctrine and discipline in the church. But this latter decree was a far cry from telling the Bishop of Rome that he should be the ruler of the western world.

Coming as it did at about the same time that the papacy was behaving at its all-time low, Valla's demonstration that the *Donation of Constantine* was a forgery was one of the last straws with which Luther broke the back of the papacy.

Martin Luther was born on November 10, 1483 — at least, that is the date his biographers generally agree on. There is, however, some doubt about that date. A few later biographers have said the year was 1484. Spalatin, a good friend of Luther's, used that year in his *Annals*. One entry in the *Table Talk* states that Luther's parents had already moved to Mansfeld when their first-born son, Martin, was born. That, too, would suggest that Luther was born in 1484. Luther's mother was sure of the day of the month, November 10, and of the time of day of her son's birth, between 11 and 12 at night. But, strangely enough, she was uncertain about the year. She, too, thought that it might have been 1484.

But Luther's brother Jacob was quoted as saying that the general impression of the Luther family afterward was that Martin was born in 1483. That was the year substantiated by the *liber decanorum*, the Dean's book at the University of Wittenberg. Modern historical research has almost uniformly accepted the year which Luther's most scholarly contemporary biographer, Melanchthon, set, namely, 1483. One thing is certain. Luther grew up in an age when exact record keeping was not in vogue.

It was a custom in that day to baptize a child, if possible, on the day following his birth. In keeping with that custom, Martin was brought to the lower tower room of St. Peter's Church in Eisleben to be baptized by Pastor Bartholomaeus Rennebacher. It was the day of the Festival of St. Martin. For that reason Hans Luther's first-born was named Martin.

Concerning the Luther family name, suffice it to say that it carries us back to the early medieval times in western Europe, to the name Lothar, or Lothaire, a name once used by a less well known emperor of the Holy Roman Empire. It seems to have found its way through the medieval centuries to the time of Luther by way of a number of spellings, such as Luder, Ludher, Lauther, Lueder, Leuder, Lutter and others. In Martin Luther's day it was quite generally spelled Luther or Lutterus.

Luther's forefathers were part of a sizeable relationship. Most of them lived either in or around the community of Moehra, an insignificant village perched in the center of Germany, in the midst of the hills of Thuringia, about eight miles from Eisenach. Boehmer, in his helpful book, *Der junge Luther*, supports the impression that the Luther relationship was a large and widespread one. He tells us that when Luther visited that area later in 1521, as a man of 38, he noted that "*sein Geschlecht nehme fast die ganze Gegend ein,"* that his relationship occupied the whole community.

Luther's ancestry itself was made up of peasants. And they remained peasants. Martin once said to Melanchthon, his closest friend in later years, "I am a peasant's son. My father, my grandfather, and all my ancestors were thorough peasants." Bainton, the familiar and prolific biographer of Luther, says that Luther's parents were sturdy, stocky, swarthy German *Bauern* — country folk. Otto Scheel, in my estimation the most detailed and most satisfying German Luther biographer, was a professor at the University of Tuebingen early in our present century. Scheel said that in his day you could still find Luther families living in the rural areas for some distance around Eisenach. Many of them, he said, even resemble pictures which we have of Luther.

The community to which we are referring was given principally to two industries, namely, agriculture and the mining of copper. These two industries seem to have rewarded the hardworking people of the community in Luther's day with moderate means for a fairly comfortable living.

When we focus our attention on the parents of Luther, in order to get a clearer picture of the home in which Luther grew up, we find ourselves in the company of unhappy biographers. There remains a lack of information about Luther's parents and the home which they maintained for their seven children — four sons and three daughters. It is hard to understand why parents of so great a son remained the objects of so little description and recorded information at the time.

7

Even Luther's *Table Talk*, written largely by Wittenberg University students who gathered regularly around Kate Luther's supper table, do not give us much information about Luther's childhood or parentage. In addition to the little we can glean from them, a few bits of information come our way from the contemporary friends and associates of Luther, such as his physician, Ratzeberger, and a student by the name of Mathesius. His closest friends and co-workers in later life, men like Spalatin and Melanchthon, occasionally recorded things which Luther revealed to them about his childhood and home-life.

Luther's father was Hans Luther (Luder), the oldest of seven children. In some other accounts we find him referred to as Grosshans (Big Hans). That was to distinguish him from Kleinhans (Little Hans), a younger brother with the same name. To have been the oldest boy in a peasant family in those days was neither all good nor all bad. For one thing, it meant that the family homestead was not a part of his inheritance. That was reserved for the youngest son, so that the parents could draw their livelihood from the income of the family holdings as long as possible. Another advantage of such an arrangement would be added security for the continuance of the inheritance of the estate within the family. But there was some advantage in this arrangement also for the older sons in the family. It lay in the fact that such an older son was free to leave his home earlier, usually as soon as he was ready to marry. More than that, it gave him the right to choose his vocation.

The vocation which Luther's father chose was mining, a vocation which was highly regarded among working people, because in many cases it led to financial prosperity. But mining, it seems, was not flourishing, as Hans would have wished it, in the Moehra area or the greater Eisleben community. It seems that too many miners had moved into the area just at the time.

For that apparent reason Hans moved with his young wife Margarethe, and his six-month-old son, Martin, to Mansfeld, about six miles away, in the region of the Harz Mountains. The first years in Mansfeld were very difficult for the young family. According to Otto Scheel, *"Sie haben es sich lassen blutsauer werden,"* things became bitterly difficult for them.

It stands to reason that it would have taken Hans some time to establish himself in the new community. Since the Luther family spoke on occasion of those early years in later life, it seems that hasty biographers of Luther nursed the impression that Martin grew up in abject poverty. Better research has proven that impression to be erroneous. It undoubtedly was encouraged by reports that Martin's mother joined other women of the community to gather wood for fuel and carried it home on her back, and that Martin, when he went off to school, sang for money in the streets. Research indicates that it was a custom for many women, even wives of the city's burghers, to carry wood from the forests on their backs to keep the home-fires glowing. And as far as the other matter is concerned, students often sang in the streets, especially where the school was connected with a religious order, as were the schools which Luther attended.

James MacKinnon writes, "The description of the straitened circumstances of the household applies at the most only to the first half-dozen years after settlement at Mansfeld." The *Table Talk* verifies these conclusions.

Some unsympathetic historians, theologians and psychiatrists have tried to find fault with the Reformer by looking for skeletons in his father's closet, but without success. The skeletons belong to Hans's younger brother, who was referred to also in the court records of Mansfeld as Kleinhans. Kleinhans was cited there frequently between the years 1499 and 1515 — eleven times, to be exact. They picture him as a man who frequented the taverns to excess and arranged deals which were usually too cleverly planned in his own favor. He was in the habit of stopping brawls by pouring beer over the head of the participant with whom his sympathies did not lie. On three occasions he dealt with his respective opponent by hitting him in the mouth, breaking a beer mug over his head, or "slapping" his hand with his sword. But during the years when these things were entered into the court records Martin was already gone from home. The years 1499-1515 cover his happy days at Eisenach, his university studies at Erfurt, his entry into the monastery and the early years of his teaching at Wittenberg University. The point is that such goings-on in Mansfeld hardly could have affected Martin very much, if indeed he knew anything at all about his wayward uncle's behavior.

There is still one story about Martin's father, Grosshans, which we want to dispel. A rumor arose that Hans once killed a man in Moehra, and that it may have been the reason for his move from Moehra to Mansfeld. The rumor does not even deserve to be called a story, because there actually is none. Its basis seems to be a flippant accusation which Luther's Catholic opponent Witzel blurted out to Luther's good friend Jonas, in the middle of a heated quarrel. Witzel said, "I might call the father of your Luther a murderer." Twenty years later an anonymous author of a polemical book which appeared in Paris actually called the Reformer "the son of the Moehra assassin." With these two exceptions, not a trace of any such story, in the writings of either friend or foe, can be found. Early in the 18th century a statement was found in a Moehra mining report that on one occasion a Hans Luther had "accidentally" killed a peasant who was minding some horses. There is, however, no authentication of the story. Nor is there any reference to such an incident in any of Luther's statements in the *Table Talk* or elsewhere. The idea that there might have been a reason like this behind Hans Luther's move to Mansfeld, which was not more than six miles from Moehra, is completely absurd in light of the excellent reputation Hans Luther quickly built up for himself there. We need to consider, too, the fact that Luther's enemies never made use of any such rumor.

The information which has come down to us concerning Luther's father leaves no doubt about the fact that he was a man of fine qualities. Melanchthon, Luther's good friend and co-worker, spoke of

Hans Luther as being a man who, by purity of character and conduct, won for himself universal affection and esteem.

The reliable record describes Hans Luther as an industrious and diligent man. When young Martin was about eight, his father Hans was already one of the leading citizens of Mansfeld. In 1491 he was named as one of four members of the city council. According to Mathesius, a pupil and early biographer of Luther, Hans ventured into the mining business for himself in 1502 and leased several mines and smelting plants. There was a common saying at that time which reflected the prosperity of the mining industry in the Mansfeld area. Some have said that Martin Luther started it. Others attribute it to Comerarius: *"Wen der Herr lieb hat, dem gibt er eine Wohnung in der Grafschaft Mansfeld"* (To the one he loves, the Lord gives a home in the county of Mansfeld). Mathesius struck the same note when he wrote that God "blessed the mining industry" of Luther's father and that Hans brought up "his son in a respectful atmosphere, using the money he had rightfully acquired as a miner."

When Martin later matriculated at the University of Erfurt, the records classified him as coming from a family of means. At about the same time his father was purchasing a respectable home in a good part of town. And when, a few years later, Martin was ordained as priest, we are told that his father rode into the monastery court with a company of twenty horsemen and then made a wealthy man's donation of 20 gold gulden to defray the expenses of the festive dinner. Though Hans Luther never became immensely wealthy, at his death he left a sizeable estate.

It has often been said that Hans Luther was an exceedingly stern man. Some recent biographers of Luther seem to be unable to probe beyond this analysis. Thus they give us an unfortunately incomplete picture of Hans. Koestlin reports in his fine biography of Luther that Hans spent long days at hard work and maintained an unusually earnest and serious tone in his household. The upright, honorable, industrious father was honestly resolved to make a useful man of his son and wanted to enable him to rise higher than himself.

It is true, too, as we learn from Luther himself, that on one occasion his father flogged him so severely that he fled from his father and bore a temporary grudge against him. Martin also said that his father's stern discipline caused him to be shy and timid during his boyhood.

But on another occasion Luther said he realized that his parents meant it for his good. Luther is quoted as often saying that in rearing children the apple should be placed next to the rod. One gets the impression that the discipline which Luther's parents carried out was not of the unloving kind which can break a child's spirit. Their strictness was well intended and proceeded from a genuine, moral earnestness of purpose.

Yes, there definitely was another side to Hans Luther. Scheel tells us in his exhaustive biography of Luther that it is totally wrong to imagine that all Martin could do was to speak of his father's strict discipline. And Koestlin relates the fact, also substantiated in the *Table Talk*, that in later life Luther often recalled in touching language the many instances of

13

his father's love. There are many testimonies to the fact that Martin loved his father dearly.

Luther's father had a considerable sense of humor. Hans and Margarethe Luther enjoyed each other's company. The whole family enjoyed singing together. Some of the jollier occasions took place, it might be said, when Hans returned home after having paused at the local tavern. Friedenthal reports that, like all miners, Hans enjoyed a good drink and sometimes returned home a little the worse for it. On these occasions, however, he never went beyond the stage of becoming pleasantly tipsy. One thing is certain — Hans was never a drunkard. His contemporaries never would have entrusted him with his responsible position or would have shown him as much respect as they did, if that had been the case.

When it comes to Margarethe, the wife of Hans Luther, we find ourselves confronted by a problem of origin. Was she Margarethe Ziegler or Margarethe Lindemann?

We have lamentably little information concerning Margarethe. Martin and his colleagues made but a few remarks about her family background.

The earliest sources mention only her first name. Luther himself gives her name simply as Margarethe. More often than not he called her by his favorite nickname, "Hanna." We have found no reason for that name. Perhaps it dates back to the time when Luther came upon the whole Bible for the first time and happened first upon the story of Hannah. He was so enthralled with it that he read it over and over again. Melanchthon, in his biographical preface to the Wittenberg edition of Luther's works, as well as

Mathesius, Luther's student and biographer, and a number of other contemporaries use only the name Margarethe. The first time we find a maiden name used is in a 1558 notice which Catherine, Luther's widow received regarding the funeral of a nephew. The second entry is in the register of Wittenberg University. On both of these occasions the name Lindemann is used, and in that latter case she is specifically described as having been "born into the family of the Lindemanns, a cognate relative of the very distinguished man, Dr. Laurentius Lindemann," a former rector of the Unversity.

In the seventeenth and eighteenth centuries a majority of biographers favored the name Lindemann. Then toward the end of the eighteenth century the consensus shifted, and it became fashionable to say that "her maiden name was Margarethe Ziegler (not Lindemann, as often given)." Half a century ago the tide turned back in favor of the name Lindemann.

In 1981 Fortress Press printed a book by Jan Siggins entitled *Luther and His Mother*. In his preface, Siggins writes confidently about how his research led him to the information which convinced him that Margarethe was indeed a Lindemann and not a Ziegler. And in the center of his book he diagrams the Lindemann family tree.

It would require a disproportionate amount of space to relate here the convincing list of facts and figures which Siggins brings forward to prove his point that Margarethe's family was one of means, one in which the men achieved responsible positions in the fields of education, politics, law and religion. The family was at home in the Eisenach area. Melanchthon said explicitly that the reason Luther was sent to school in Eisenach was that "his mother had been born there of an old and respected family." In 1520 Luther said, "Almost all of my kinsfolk are at Eisenach" and that there one person would call him "nephew," another "uncle," another "maternal cousin." Heinrich Schalbe, with whom Luther spent much time while at school in Eisenach is described as the mayor of the city and a relative of the Lindemanns. In his first extant letter Luther invites Vicar Braun to his first mass in Erfurt in 1507 and expresses gratitude to the "Schalbe College, those excellent people who, from my point of view, are as richly deserving as they could possibly be."

On the other hand, it is reported that the Zieglers were a farm family in Moehra. They were not cottagers from the landless ranks of poor peasant laborers, but landholders like Hans Luther's parents with respectable assets. If Hans Luther would have married Margarethe Ziegler it would not have been said, as it was, that Hans Luther "married above his rank."

At this point someone may ask why so much is made of the question as to whether Margarethe was a Ziegler or a Lindemann. First of all, Melanchthon tells us that Martin was "diligently instructed at home in the knowledge and fear of God" as soon as he could understand. He also notes that his mother's own modesty, fear of God, and prayerfulness were especially obvious and that other women paid attention to her as an example of virtue. We hear, too, that Luther demonstrated great skill in language and music at an early age. Some hastily prepared biographies give credit for all of this to Ursula

Cotta and do not consider the possibility that it was his skill in singing that attracted her attention to begin with. Furthermore, to give Frau Cotta credit for his fine language and correct manners — as though all of this could have been accomplished in fewer than three years — is to give her credit for a most remarkable, perhaps unbelievable, achievement. That will become all the more clear when we talk about his stay at Eisenach and notice how busy the years were for Martin while he was at school and staying with the Schalbes and Vicar Braun.

Aside from all of this, what sort of person was Margarethe, or Hanna, Luther? Melanchthon, who came to know Margarethe very well and grew very fond of her, described her as "a worthy woman, distinguished for her many virtues, above all for her modesty, her fear of God, and her constant communion with God in prayer." Elsewhere Melanchthon spoke of her admiringly, saying that she was "held in high esteem by other respectable women as an example of a virtuous life."

Spalatin, Luther's good friend since college days and court preacher and secretary to Elector Frederick the Wise of Saxony, spoke of her as a "rare and exemplary woman." Several biographers tell of the little ditty which she would repeat occasionally to her husband. It went like this:

> *Mir und dir ist keiner hold,*
> *das ist unser beider Schuld.*

A prosaic translation would be, "It's our own fault if people don't like us."

Swiss Kessler tells us that both Hans and Margarethe were small and short, and that their son Martin far surpassed them in height and build. They were dark-complexioned. Cranach's familiar portraits of them depict a certain hardness in their features, perhaps a reflection of their labor and toil. The mother looks more wearied by life, but resigned, quiet and meditative. Her thin face, with its large bones, presents a mixture of mildness and gravity. Spalatin, at first sight of her, was amazed to see how much Luther resembled her in his bearing and features.

There is a story, frequently repeated, that on one occasion Margarethe beat her son until blood came, merely because he stole a single nut. The many other reports about Margarethe make it seem likely that the "nut" story is at worst an exaggeration. MacKinnon, another of Luther's biographers, wrote, ". . . nor was his mother always scolding and thrashing her young brood." Luther himself told of the jovial way in which his mother played with her children. MacKinnon reports further that the atmosphere of the Luther home in which she was ever present was a pious one. The children were taught by precept and example the fear of God and the religious usages of the time. In his fine biography of Luther, Scheel says that it is simply wrong to think of Martin's childhood as being unhappy.

The people in Germany during the time that Luther was a child attributed many of their misfortunes to witchcraft. It was true of mostly everyone, regardless of walk of life or social station. But it was more true among the rural folks who thought that the witches worked through the forces of nature, especially through the destruction of storms. Luther's mother certainly was no exception to the rule. Luther often spoke in later years of the many things his parents had to say about the activities of devils, witches and other unwholesome powers. When one of Luther's little brothers died, his mother is said to have cried out against a neighbor woman who she thought was a witch and had caused the little boy's death. Luther's father is said to have come home from the mine one evening to report that one of his workers in the mine had been killed that day, and that it had been the work of a witch. Some of his contemporaries claimed that the sacraments had been given to the church to thwart the work of witches.

Before we leave the home of young Luther, there is one rumor we ought to address, if only for the reason that some of his enemies were spreading it. In a frustrated, last-ditch effort to convince people that Luther was the forerunner of the Antichrist, his enemies decided to slander his mother. They alleged that before Margarethe's marriage to Hans Luther, she had served as a maid in the public baths of Eisleben. There she was supposed to have yielded to the attention of an *incubus*, a demoniac visitor, by whom she conceived her firstborn son, Martin. For quite a while a heated pamphlet debate raged concerning this ugly story between the enemies of Luther and his admiring defenders. This debate seems to have reached its climax about the time of Luther's vital debate with Eck at Leipzig in 1519, when unscrupulous enemies like Eck and other Dominicans were doing their utmost to discredit the upstart reformer.

Luther himself twice refuted the unfortunate attack on the integrity of his parents, according to the

Table Talk. A number of trustworthy men, like
Mathesius and Spangenberg, wrote sermons and
treatises in opposition to Luther's enemies. Coelius,
an ardent admirer of Luther, went so far as to com-
pare Luther with Elijah, John the Baptist and Jere-
miah. And Dr. Bugenhagen, Luther's long-time co-
worker and admirer, when delivering the German
sermon at Luther's funeral on Febrary 22, 1546, said
of Luther that he was the angel of Revelation 14:7
who flies through the heaven with the eternal gospel
to proclaim to those on earth. Apart from all de-
fenses, the slanderous remarks against Luther's
mother in the course of time were bound to collapse
under the weight of their own foolishness.

CHAPTER TWO

Early Education

The first school Luther attended was in the middle of the village of Mansfeld. There is a question about his exact age at the time he started school, but it appears that he must have started when exceptionally young. The school at Mansfeld was one of the many "Latin" schools which were established to prepare students for a higher education. The suggested time for starting such a school was when a boy had reached seven. It seems, however, that Luther started at an earlier age. Melanchthon recalled that Luther told him he had been so young and small that an older friend, Nicolaus Oemler, had to take him up in his arms and carry him to school. That hardly would have been necessary in the case of a seven-year-old boy, especially since the school was but a few blocks from the Luther home. Moreover, the oldest record states that Luther first entered school on St. George's Day, March 12, 1488, when he was four-and-a-half years old.

What kind of a school was it at Mansfeld, and how did Luther fare at that school? Luther gives us the impression that he heartily disliked the Mansfeld school. He later called it "an asses' stable, a hell and a purgatory." He complained about the whip, large as a broom, which was used for disciplining. He even went so far as to write, "We were martyrized there."

These comments were written in 1524, twenty-seven years after his days at Mansfeld and three years after the Diet of Worms. At that particular time the enrollment at Wittenberg, where Luther was teaching university courses, had fallen markedly. It was widely known that Luther favored humanistic courses for his university. All of the other German universities were still steeped in scholasticism, as were those of Italy and France. When Luther noticed that the enrollment had decreased to about a third its former size, he decided to address a treatise to all the city councillors of Germany regarding the state of affairs in their schools. In that document he made the remarks quoted above and other similar statements. What he really was trying to do was to discredit the scholastic schools, of which Mansfeld had been a seedbed in the days when he attended it. The humanistic schools which Luther knew and in which he had some influence were still in that early phase of humanism which encouraged the study of the classics so that the students could read the Scriptures in the orginal Greek and Hebrew. Luther felt that it was time to use strong language in the war against scholasticism, and, to quote Schwiebert, "at that he was an artist."

Mansfeld was a *trivial Schule*, one of the schools whose purpose was to teach the *trivium*, the first three of the elementary liberal arts taught in medieval schools. The *trivium* consisted of grammar, rhetoric, and dialectic (the application of logic). The other four of the seven liberal arts, the *quadrivium*, which were to be taught in the higher schools, were geometry, astronomy, arithmetic and music.

Critics of Mansfeld claimed that the school did not teach the whole *trivium*. Luther himself, in his critical moments, complained that he got very little religion at the school and no history — that all that he got was Latin and music. Otto Scheel in his biography of Luther gives us a different picture. He tells us that while it is true that Mansfeld did not formally include all of the *trivium*, the school did teach a thorough course in Latin. Its literature courses in connection with rhetoric included authors like Cato, Aesop, Boethius, Plautus and Terence — a palette so rich in history and culture that it was bound to produce well-rounded and well-educated graduates. Though there were few religion courses at Mansfeld, the endless masses, meditations, processions, singing and applications in other courses, gave Luther a much better background than his average contemporaries received in religion. When you add to all of this the benefit of the music his mother had taught him, especially religious music, and the understanding she was able to impart in the area of religion, young Martin must have been very well equipped. The records at Erfurt and later at Wittenberg show plainly that the boys who matriculated at these schools with Mansfeld backgrounds came well prepared. Luther was one of the leaders among them.

On the other hand, at a *trivial Schule* like the one in Mansfeld there were customs which educators in subsequent times and certainly today would condemn outright. Two illustrations will suffice. First, there was the *lupus*, or wolf, slate. Each time a student lapsed from Latin into German or used profanity his name was written on a slate, and he was called a *lupus*. Every eight days the slate was checked. Each boy was then spanked in keeping with the number of times his name appeared there. The other illustration involves the *asinus*, the wooden donkey. At the end of a recitation or when an examination was graded, the student at the bottom of the class was required to hang a tiny wooden donkey around his neck. And every time a boy had to wear the *asinus* his name was also added to the slate — injury on top of insult. One morning Luther was spanked 15 times for not knowing his Latin declension — a punishment he must have accumulated over a period of eight days.

Practices like this were encouraged by the parents and the city councils. Most schools had well defined systems of punishment. Parents who objected to the type of punishment used in a particular school were not permitted to enroll their children there. It is interesting to note that while Luther was occasionally spanked for faulty declensions and conjugations, the gentle and precocious Melanchthon received daily spankings during his days at school in Pforzheim. One comtemporary complained that Latin was not really taught in that school system, but rather was pounded into the students.

When the boys grew larger and spankings were more difficult to administer, the offenders were subjected to fines. This system was referred to as *Geldbussen* and remained in vogue in German schools for many years.

In all likelihood it was during the Easter season of 1497 that Luther left Mansfeld in order to enter the

Cathedral school at Magdeburg. It so happened that a good friend and schoolmate, Johann Reinecke, the son of a well-to-do blast furnace superintendent in Mansfeld, made the same transfer at this time, and Martin decided to go with him. The two men remained close friends for the rest of their lives.

Melanchthon tells us that it was Luther's father who sent him to Magdeburg since by now Luther's father was enjoying financial success and liked the idea of his son's being in the company of the son of the wealthy Reinecke. Mathesius, on the other hand, tells us that it was Martin's wish to enroll at Magdeburg since that school enjoyed a reputation "far above many others." The reason might well have been a combination of the above. Otto Scheel gives Luther's father Hans credit for the decision. He knew about the fine reputation of the Magdeburg school and proudly decided it was to be the one for his son. Scheel further explains that Magdeburg was easier to reach than the other renowned schools which Hans might have considered.

It also should be said that it was a custom for young men who sought a higher education to enroll at a variety of *trivial Schulen*, one at a time, before picking their university. They were known as wandering students. While the seven fine arts, the *trivium* and *quadrivium*, filled the curriculum at the *trivial Schulen*, each school had its particular strong suit. By attending several of them a student hoped to prepare himself as well as possible for entry into the university.

The city of Magdeburg at the time had a population of 12,000. It was filled with endowed churches and chapels, where the clergy were continually reading masses. Many of the monastic orders of the day were represented in the city. The *Dom*, or cathedral, of Magdeburg stood at the center of all this activity. In the large area behind the cathedral stood the Mosshaus, the palace of the Archbishop, and the famous cathedral school.

Magdeburg was also a storehouse of relics, which the clergy paraded through the streets in processions on the Mondays after Easter and Pentecost. Palm Sunday and Ascension Day were also the occasion for colorful processions. The body of the patron saint Florentius was entombed in the chancel of the cathedral. On his birthday his remains were brought out into the nave. One can hardly deny the impression this "Little Rome" must have made on the young Luther.

It was here that Luther had another experience which he recalled several times in his writings and conversations. It may have contributed to his sudden decision later on to enter a monastery. Prince William of Anhalt, a patron of the Franciscan Order, walked through the streets of Magdeburg barefooted and begging alms. He had fasted to the point where he looked like a dead man, with nothing but skin and bones. He died soon after Luther first saw him. All who looked on this illustrious figure in such a pitiful state were deeply moved by the spectacle and felt ashamed of their way of life.

Luther never mentioned exactly which school he attended in Magdeburg. There were several to choose from. But he did say that he studied under Brethren of the Common Life, usually referred to as the *Nullbrueder* (the zero, or nothing, brothers), so called because of their *lollen*, or soft singing. Their order had been founded by Gerhard Groote, who hailed from the Netherlands. They were forerunners of the mystics and were known for their Bible-reading and their preaching that both the clergy and laity should return to a simple, pious way of life. They did not have a school of their own at Magdeburg, but the Archbishop did permit a group of them to teach in the cathedral school. It is for that reason that Luther scholars generally agree that Luther attended that particular school. This information leads us to another interesting possibility, namely, that it was in Magdeburg in the Bible-reading atmosphere of the *Nullbrueder*, rather than later in Erfurt, that Luther discovered the whole Bible for the first time.

Since Luther spent only one year in Magdeburg, many biographers pass over it as if it were of little if any importance. It is possible that quite the opposite was the case, considering Magdeburg's strong monastic message, its cathedral atmosphere, the Bible-reading influence of the mystics, the *Nullbrueder*, and the likelihood of Luther's discovery of the full Bible for the first time. It may well have been a pivotal year for the Reformer-in-the-making.

It was Easter time in 1498 when Luther's parents suddenly decided that he should change schools in favor of finishing his preparatory education in the *trivial Schule* at Eisenach. Eisenach, a beautiful little city of about 4,000, was nestled in the Thuringian Hills, near the Wartburg Castle. Melanchthon and Matheson claim that Luther was sent there because his mother had been born there into an old and respected family. Luther himself remarked in later life that he had been sent to Eisenach because "almost all of my kinsfolk on my mother's side were at Eisenach."

Again the question arises as to who Luther's mother actually was, whether she was a Ziegler or a Lindemann. If the latter is true, then it becomes easy to understand why the Reformer often reflected on his three years in Eisenach as the best years of his life. For in that case he was living among illustrious relatives. The Lindemanns, Schalbes and Cottas were interrelated and were all part of the same circle of Eisenach patricians. Then it also becomes easy to understand his saying that it was "not for penury, but because it was tradition, that a student would sing" in the streets. Cultured and fairly wealthy relatives took care of him in their homes.

It seems that it was in the home of Heinrich Schalbe, his uncle and a wealthy burger and son of a mayor of Eisenach, that Martin received most of his meals, while he lived in the home of Kuntz and Ursula Cotta. He also became well acquainted with his mother's uncle, Johannes Braun, vicar of St. Mary's, whose love for poetry and music and whose broader cultural interests attracted his curiosity. Vicar Braun also seems to have represented the Schalbe family's interest in the Franciscan monastery which the family had established at the foot of the Wartburg, just outside Eisenach. And so he frequently brought young Luther into contact with the monks of that institution, known as the *Barfuesser Kloster*, the Barefooted Cloister. It is said that the young Luther, serious and pious beyond his years, expressed so much interest in the priesthood that on one occasion Ursula Cotta told him that nothing was dearer on earth than the love of a woman to him who could win it. Perhaps she shared some of Hans Luther's reservations about the monastic life.

When in later years Luther expressed his appreciation of the school at Eisenach, he referred to it as the "Schalbe College" and to his relatives and friends there as "those excellent people who from my point of view are as richly deserving as they could possibly be." Elsewhere he is quoted as saying that the three years at his "beloved Eisenach" were among the most pleasant of his life.

In spring of 1501, when Luther was not quite eighteen, he began his university studies. Erfurt was his chosen school. Although Luther's father still had several children to care for at home, business had been so good that he felt sure he could raise the money for his oldest son's prolonged stay at the university. Hans and Margarethe thought the matter over carefully and agreed that he should enroll at Erfurt. Martin was happy with the decision. Higher education had obviously been his goal, in view of his curriculum at Magdeburg and Eisenach.

But how did it happen that he chose to attend Erfurt? Some say that the Luthers liked the proximity of Erfurt to Mansfeld. But that is not true. The Leipzig University would have been closer. We are told that Erfurt had a good reputation among the universities of Germany, better even than that of Leipzig at the time. If Luther had enrolled at Leipzig, which seems to have been the most likely alternative, there may never have been a Reformation. Leipzig was and remained a school ardently loyal to the papacy. It was the school at which the brilliant John

Eck would engage Luther in debate a few years later. It was a Dominican school. The pope considered it one of his strongholds north of the Alps. If Luther had enrolled at Leipzig, he might have become a monk, but it is almost certain he never would have become an Augustinian, but rather a Dominican. The Augustinians were encouraged to study the Scriptures, while the Dominicans steeped themselves in scholastic philosophy.

The best estimates place the population of the city of Erfurt at about 20,000. It was a typical medieval city. It had no definite street plan. Streets were crooked and narrow and often led to dead ends. Footbridges spanned the many hazardous streams and canals. There was no street illumination, and therefore a minimum of night life in the city.

Countless church activities caused Erfurt, like Magdeburg, to be described as a "little Rome." There were, besides the cathedral, two endowed churches, 22 cloisters, 23 cloister churches, 36 chapels, and 6 hospitals. Every order of monasticism was represented in the city. Majestic rites and colorful processions were almost a daily experience. In later years Luther recalled how he participated in many of these rites.

And these were not all the things which kept Luther in a constant atmosphere of things monastic and priestly. When students enrolled at some German universities they had to join a fraternity house, known as a *bursa*, or burse. The social standing of a student was closely related to the reputation of the burse to which he belonged. If a student was not accepted into any burse, he was forced to leave the school. The burse to which Luther belonged at Erfurt was that of St. George, the dragon-killer. His roommate during part of his stay at Erfurt was Crotus Rubeanus. Historians are still holding Crotus under suspicion of being one of the extremely clever and satiric authors of the *Letters of Obscure Men.*

Two of Luther's best Erfurt friends were Spalatin and Carlstadt. Spalatin later became a priest, too, and secretary to Elector Frederic the Wise. Thus he was able to recommend Luther for a position on the Wittenberg faculty. Carlstadt later joined the faculty at Wittenberg with Luther, but during Luther's absence at the Wartburg he turned radical and became a source of irritation to the Reformation.

The burse system at Erfurt was tied closely to the church. Imagine a present-day fraternity at one of our universities run according to strict monastic rules. It meant that Luther had to live in crowded quarters and under a special discipline borrowed from the monastery. The students wore dignified uniforms of semi-clerical design with a rapier, a long, slender two-edged sword with a cuplike hilt, at the side. There was strict supervision — up at 4:00 a.m., to bed at 8:00 p.m. Lectures, seminars and disputations were compulsory and began at 6:00 a.m. Otto Scheel tells us that the food was good and light beer was plentiful. Each burse had its own homemade beer. The master of the burse always kept the key to the beer supply room. The cook and the brewer received a high salary.

Contacts with the outside world, especially occasions for meeting with women, were strictly controlled. Places which the students frequented were always supervised. Leaving the burse in the evening was difficult. It meant checking out a lantern from the rector's office and returning it immediately upon return.

Under these closely-supervised circumstances during his nearly-four-year stay at Erfurt, Luther maintained an excellent record. Such information helps us set aside some of the accusations which his enemies later tried to bring against his character. The university gave him a high recommendation.

There are those who suggest that Luther's behavior at Erfurt may have been immoral and that it was his guilt that later drove him into the monastery and led him to his conclusions about "justification by faith alone." We will explore the doctrine itself later, but for now it is enough to note that Scheel, Boehmer and Strohl, three of the most dependable and thorough Luther scholars, have critically examined every existing source and have found absolutely no support for the accusations which Luther's enemies leveled against him.

The initiation of fraternity members included a friendly program of humiliation, politely referred to as a deposition. When, as an upper-classman at Erfurt, Luther was given the honor of making a deposition speech for the reception of the new members, he traced in a humorous way the etymology of the word *deponere* and spoke of that aspect of the initiation. In later life he spoke of his youthful deposition at Erfurt as being good training for the heavier depositions of life.

When Luther enrolled at Erfurt, the university was enjoying an enrollment of 2,000 and the distinction of being one of the largest universities in Germany, if not in Europe. It was one of the old, well-established universities of Europe. That may have been one of the things which encouraged Luther to enroll there. Upon his enrollment Luther entered the Liberal Arts Department to prepare for his Bachelor of Arts Degree. He had to spend considerable time reviewing the *trivium* and then expanding his study of the *quadrivium*. When he applied for the Bachelor's examination, he swore that he had read extensively in the fields of grammar, logic and rhetoric, natural philosophy, spheric astronomy, philosophy and psychology. Melanchthon implied later that Luther's education at this point might have been carried out more effectively had they let his genius at once master all of the arts and sciences instead of burdening him with "thorny dialectics." Still, when we now review the Reformation career of Luther we cannot avoid the opinion that this early training in dialectics prepared him well for the literary battles and debates which lay ahead. Fortunately, the curriculum at Erfurt was such that a young man with primarily religious leanings would receive every conceivable encouragement.

The philosophy of the faculty at Erfurt during Luther's four years there seems to have been in the process of change. The day of scholasticism's great popularity and the great admiration for Thomas Acquinas and Duns Scotus and the *via antiqua*, the "old way," was on its way out. The scholastic theologians had gone out of their way to try to harmonize pagan philosophy, notably Aristotle's, with Christian revelation, as was evidenced especially by Thomas Acquinas's lengthy *Summa Theologica*. The *via moderna*, or "new way," of William Ockham

and others had come to the fore, with its conten-
tion that human reason is of no avail in the realm
of faith. In fact, they separated philosophy into
two realms. In the realm of faith, revelation could
be the only guide; but in the matters of this world,
human reason should be used to its fullest extent.

Luther for a time called Ockham his "Master"
and accepted without question the philosophical
lead of his Erfurt professors. During his four years
at Erfurt a long list of Europe's acknowledged
scholars lectured at Erfurt for a season and then
moved on. The two of them who stayed the longest
won Luther's affection. He often spoke of them in
later years. One was Trutvetter, an able professor
who deplored the hair-splitting argumentation of
the scholastics. He also tried to simplify the dialectics of Ockham. This may have been one of the
reasons why Luther liked him. Luther did study
Aristotle's works on logic, ethics, physics and metaphysics, with modern applications. He believed, as
did his teacher, that the world is a sphere. This
was, of course, in the wake of Christopher Colum-
bus's travels. The other professor whom Luther appreciated very much at the time was Usingen, a
second Ockhamist who seems to have had great
influence on Luther during these years. In theology
he distinguished between Aristotle and the Bible.
In matters of faith he accepted the Scriptures as an
unerring guide to truth. It has been said that Usingen may have sowed the *sola scriptura* conviction
in Luther and that his criticism of scholasticism
may have had much to do with Luther's throwing the

scholastic philosophy out of his Wittenberg window later on.

Some say that Luther became a humanist at Erfurt, but their claim does not bear up under most research. It is true that humanism came to Erfurt toward the close of his Erfurt stay, but Luther never became a humanist in the full sense of the term. The only reason he appeared to some as being a humanist was because he avidly read the Latin classics. But he did this mainly for the sake of language study. In later years he reportedly said that the curriculum at Erfurt was simply too heavy to allow him to read enough to become a humanist. That statement infers that he might have liked to do so. We are told that when he packed to leave for the monastery he did sell or give away all of his law books. He also disposed of his beloved lute. But he did take with him his well-worn copies of the classic Latin authors, Virgil, Plautus, Cicero and Livy!

Examinations for the Bachelor of Arts Degree were announced each fall and spring. Anyone, depending on the preliminary training with which he had come to Erfurt, could apply to take the examination. Most students would take it as soon as they could in order to get started on their Master's program. Luther had been at Erfurt one year plus one summer when in the fall of 1502 he took the examination and earned his Bachelor's Degree. He ranked 30th in a class of 57. None of the sources reveal any explanation for his less than stellar showing — not even in the top half of his class. One wonders what the reason might have been, after reading so much about his diligence and hearing of how even modern analysts judge him to have been an incomparable genius. One explanation offers itself on the surface. It may be that Luther took his examination prematurely, that because of all his other reading he did not review the required materials as completely as he should have. The Bachelor's Degree qualified Luther for some teaching at the university. So while he began the courses for his Master's Degree he assisted with the teaching of grammar and logic.

The courses he studied in preparation for the Bachelor's Degree, we recall, were known as the *trivium* and consisted of grammar, rhetoric and logic. To these the student, if diligent, would add physics and philosophy. Now, in preparation for the Master's Degree, the student concentrated on the *quadrivium*, namely, music, arithmetic, geometry and astronomy. Here, too, if the student was diligent, he would add courses like general mathematics, metaphysics and ethics. The question is asked at times if any attention was given to other subjects which are common in university curricula today, such as literature, history and geography. Subjects like these were considered background material all the way through. The students were expected to review them in preparation for their examinations.

In early 1505, as soon as the required time period elapsed since he had received his Bachelor's Degree, Luther received his Master's Degree. This time he fared much better and ranked second in a class of seventeen. He had now earned both of his preliminary degrees in the shortest allowable time. It was a goal which only the most gifted and dedicated students were able to accomplish.

Martin's father was, of course, extremely proud of the oldest son. To be sure, he was making further plans for his son. Since he had long known what it meant to earn one's way by the sweat of the brow, Hans urged his son to begin the study of law. For centuries law had been the royal road to advancement for sons of the bourgeoisie, and he planned that Martin, too, should follow this pathway to success in the world of practical affairs. Law was the profession most highly regarded by nearly everyone in that day. Perhaps Martin could even find his way into politics and attain to some position of power and wealth on the European scene. Now that Hans himself had climbed the ladder far enough so that he could afford it, he let his decision be known by buying his brilliant son a costly edition of the *Corpus Iuris Civilis*, a huge three-part text and training book in law which had been the authentic and official sources for law study ever since the days of Emperor Justinian. They often were referred to as Rome's greatest gift to posterity. More than that, Hans Luther's heart, nearly bursting with pride and ambition, wanted one more thing for the young man. In fact, he already had picked out a socially acceptable bride for his illustrious son.

Martin himself was, of course, very happy about his academic achievements. When in later years he spoke of the day in 1505 when he earned his Master's Degree, he said, "What a moment of majesty and splendor that was when one took the degree of Master, and torches were carried before him and everyone paid him honor! I consider that no temporal or worldly joy can equal it." Melanchthon tells us, on the authority of several of Luther's fellow students, that his talent was already at that time the wonder of the whole university.

CHAPTER THREE

FROM THE MONASTERY TO THE CLASSROOM

After Martin Luther received his Master of Arts degree in the spring of 1505, there were three months before the lectures in law at Erfurt University were to begin. It was during this time that people who were close to Martin began to notice a change in him. He seemed to be given to periods of melancholy and deep thought. What might the cause of this difference be in one who so recently had experienced happy moments and the joy of life characteristic of the students at Erfurt University, especially during the days of graduation? Could it be that he was unhappy about the very thing which was making his father proud and happy, namely, the fact that he was about to enroll in law school?

Now that Martin had a little time to reflect, his many, many contacts with priests and monasteries returned to his memory. Every school which he had attended, from Mansfeld through Magdeburg, Eisenach and Erfurt, had been completely immersed in the activities and atmosphere of the church.

When the time came, however, for the lectures in law to start, Martin was at hand and enrolled. From

43

no one do we get the impression that he enjoyed or even remotely liked his new curriculum. We recall that when Luther had pondered the question as to which course he should take after getting his Master's Degree, there were really only three possibilities at Erfurt: medicine, theology and law. And of these only law was open to him, for there was no one enrolling in medicine that term, and theology would have required celibacy of him. To that his father never would have agreed.

Soon followed the incident which is familiar to everyone who knows even only a little about Luther. His study of law had lasted only five weeks when Martin seems to have felt the need for some time off. He traveled home to Mansfeld to see his parents. He made the journey on foot, which gave him plenty of time to think. It was June 30 when he started his trip back to Erfurt. On July 2, when he had come within a few miles of Erfurt, he was suddenly overtaken by a severe thunderstorm. He sought shelter under a tree near Stotternheim. Suddenly the tree was struck by a bolt of lightning, and Luther was thrown to the ground. Once again he was overcome by the fear which had long been nagging at him, the fear of sudden death. Intense feelings of guilt arose from his consciousness of sin. Gripped by fear he cried out, "Help me, St. Anna! and I will become a monk!" Martin had learned to pray to St. Anna, since she was the patron saint of miners, and therefore of his father.

Luther believed implicitly that his oath to St. Anna was binding on him in the sight of God. Unless he should be granted a dispensation, it was his duty to fulfill it. Certain that there was a divine message for him in the storm, he was determined to bow to God's will.

Two weeks later, on July 16, he invited his friends from the burse of St. Mary's, his law school fraternity, to a farewell party in one of the Erfurt inns which was frequented by students with their female acquaintances. Here he revealed the carefully kept secret concerning his plans to enter a monastery. The next day, July 17, he made his way across town to the Augustinian monastery. When the gate of the monastery opened, Luther bade farewell to his friends who had accompanied him. They tried their best to dissuade him, but he replied, "Today you see me, but after this never." They left in tears, while Martin Luther disappeared behind the gates.

Why did Luther follow through on his decision to enter the monastery? When we consider his serious nature; his contemplation of sin, death and judgment; his regular contact with priests and monks wherever he attended school; his ardent love for theology and the classics, fields for which his present study of law left no time; and how all of this worked on him until that night in the storm — we can appreciate the conclusion of Heinrich Boehmer in his Book, *Der junge Luther*. Boehmer writes, "We can safely claim that inwardly Luther was already on the road to the monastery when the lightning at Stotternheim crashed down on him. The hysterical fear that came over him in that moment only hastened the decision; it did not create the attitude of mind out of which the decision was made."

Luther also had had two other recent brushes with death and found them hard to forget. In the spring of 1502, the spring before he received his Bachelor's Degree, while traveling home during the Easter recess, he accidentally cut the main artery in one of his legs with his rapier. This happened about an hour's distance from Erfurt. While a friend who was traveling with him ran for a doctor, he pressed the wound tightly as he lay on his back with his leg lifted in the air. The leg began to swell and the doctor, it seems, was a bungler. By the time they managed to get Luther back to Erfurt, he had lost so much blood that he was growing faint. He called upon St. Mary for help and then lost consciousness. A few nights later the wound broke open again, and again he cried out, "O Mary, help me!" Veit Dietrich quotes him later as saying, "If I had died at that time, I would have died in the name of Mary."

It happened, too, that during that same period which we are talking about, one of Luther's best friends died suddenly. There is some difference among biographers as to who that friend was, as well as to the manner of his death. Melanchthon said he knew of the incident but did not know the circumstances. But he did add that the incident made as great an impression on the young Luther as did the electrical storm. Mathesius claims that this good friend was a man by the name of Alexius, and that he had been stabbed. Mathesius felt that this incident, too, had a devastating effect on Luther. There was still one more tragedy in the circle of Luther's friends at Erfurt at the time, namely, the death of one Hieronymus Buntz, who succumbed to pleurisy.

In Luther's day many of the monastic orders were the objects of criticism and ridicule because of idleness, hypocrisy and immorality. Nevertheless, many serious young men were still attracted by the thought of pleasing God through the solemn renunciation of marriage and of this world's goods. The church firmly taught that absolute submission to the regulations of a monastic order constituted true service to God and raised the participants to a peculiar position of holiness and merit. In fact, it was said to young men who were pondering the possibility of joining that the vows would furnish the new monk with the blessings of a new baptism. Luther tells us that he received the same assurance. The Luther of later years declared that his monastic vow was a compulsory one, illegitimately forced from him by terror and the fear of death.

Why did Luther wait two weeks after the storm at Stotternheim before entering the monastery? We know that he did not go home to tell his parents in person. Was it purely for the sake of thinking matters over or to seek further advice at Erfurt? Luther himself tells us that priests and personal friends, especially Vicar Braun, voiced their opposition. The most obvious answer is that Luther wanted to set his house in order and to bid farewell to his friends.

But what was Hans's reaction to Martin's decision? According to the prevailing law, Martin was not bound to procure his father's consent for his entrance into a monastery. To Martin, however, it seemed utterly impossible that he should take such a step without their knowledge, and he wanted their approbation. So before the 17th of July, the day he made his application for admission, he sent a message to inform his parents of his intentions and to ask their blessing. The answer which he received from Mansfeld shortly after July 17 exceeded even his worst apprehensions. Boehmer tells us that his father acted like a madman. After Martin had received his Master's Degree, Hans had begun to address his son with *Ihr*, the pronoun of respect for one's superior or elder. Now he promptly reverted to addressing him with *du*, the common word for "you." He told him that he had lost all paternal grace and favor. His mother and the rest of his relatives also let him know that they would have nothing more to do with him. Martin was confronted by a dreadfully difficult choice, either to break with his family for good or to go against his vow back into the world. Then, unexpectedly, a second letter arrived from Mansfeld relieving him of the dreaded choice. At the last moment his father gave in. This dramatic change on his father's part is usually attributed to the fact that Hans's two younger sons died suddenly of the plague and that a rumor reached him that Martin, too, had been stricken by the disease. When the rumor proved to be false, friends and acquaintances told the hot-tempered father that he was in duty bound to "offer something holy to God." So he gave in, though "with reluctance and sadness." As time went by, Hans's attitude toward Martin became steadily more conciliatory.

Why, of all monastic orders, did Luther choose the Augustinian Eremites? Even in the comparatively small city of Erfurt there were no fewer than six orders. In addition to the Augustinians at the Augustan Gate, there were the Benedictine Abbey on Peter's Hill, the Carthusians in the southern part of the city, the convent of the Dominicans on the left bank of the

48

Broad Creek, the Franciscans on the right bank and the little cloister of Servites, or "Servants of the Holy Virgin," at the Kraempfer Gate. The "Black Cloister," the one which Luther chose, was not far from Lehmann's Bridge in the northeastern part of the city. But why this cloister?

Luther never answers that question for us directly. But knowing Luther's state of mind at the time, and knowing something about the Black Cloister, the reason becomes apparent. For one thing, the cloister in Erfurt belonged to the most important Augustinian Order in Germany. It was considered the foremost center for cultivating the ascetic ideal, and therefore enjoyed the greatest prestige. It was said that among the Augustinians at Erfurt Luther could hope soonest to reach the goal of "evangelical perfection." To what extent Luther knew at this point the thoughts and writings of Augustine we cannot say, but it is reasonable to suppose that after his four years of university training he knew them well. Luther simply may have wanted to follow in the footsteps of Augustine. Schaff-Herzog adds the observation that the Thuringo-Saxon province of the Augustinian Order boasted some of the most famous theologians of the day. Among them were members of the Erfurt faculty. Professor Proles, for example, had founded the congregation of Observantine Eremites according to strictest principles; another instructor was Johann Staupitz; and still another was von Paltz, a then-famous lecturer and pulpit orator. Furthermore, Luther did not just join the Augustinians, but chose the Observantines, who were bent on observing all

49

of the strictest principles of the Order. Luther knew what he was looking for.

There is still another matter which may have had something to do with Luther's choosing the Augustinian Order. While it is true that the Augustinian Eremites, or Hermits, were a mendicant, or begging, order, the Erfurt monastery was so wealthy that its inmates had long since ceased to beg for a living. They no longer recruited from the lower classes but rather from the middle and higher classes of the population. Illiterates were admitted only as monks of the second class, as *fratres*, or lay brothers, who were expected to perform the menial tasks. Only the monks of the first class were entitled to vote and were known as *patres*, or fathers. These included educated men and clerics who occupied themselves largely with singing, praying and other ascetic practices.

The Augustinians were very cautious about accepting a new member into their fold. When Luther first applied for membership on July 17 he was not admitted at once. He was first assigned to the monastic hostelry for observation of the state of his soul. The authorities wanted to assure themselves that "his spirit was of God." He had to be given the opportunity, as a guest of the monastery, to examine himself earnestly to see whether he could endure the "harshness" of the Order and abide in his purpose.

So it was not until early September, a month and a half later, that his reception took place in the monastery church with the customary formalities. There on the steps of the altar sat the prior, before whom Luther prostrated himself. Then the prior asked, "What do you desire?" Luther replied, "God's grace and mercy." Thereupon the novice was raised from the floor and asked by the prior if he were married, had any attachments or any disease. Then he was reminded of the severity of the Order and asked whether he could undergo all such hardships with the help of God. During the singing of the hymn, "Great Father Augustine," he removed his secular attire in favor of his *Moenchsgewand*, his monks' attire. In the meanwhile, the prior chanted the words, "The Lord attire you in the new man."

The new habit whch Luther now wore was basically a white house-dress. Over it he wore a black scapular, a sleeveless cloth vestment, falling to the floor in front and back. The latter was held in place with a leather belt. He was to wear this garb at all times, even while sleeping. Because of this garment the Augustinian cloister in Erfurt, like its counterpart in Wittenberg, was also called the Black Cloister.

Some accounts give the impression that Luther spent a lot of time doing menial tasks, hoping that such behavior might bring him to the realization of his much-sought-after peace of mind, the "new baptism." Some of these accounts give the impression that the older monks ridiculed him for his diligence. Scheel tells us that these oft-repeated reports are grossly exaggerated and do not ring true to the record. We are expressly told that at the beginning, at least, the university interceded on his behalf as a member of their own body for his exemption from such tasks. In later years Luther never complained about any such vexations and burdens.

It is true, of course, that while he was a novice he was obliged to learn how, when and where to bend the knee, to throw himself to the ground, to walk around with eyes downcast, to refrain from laughter and speaking. He did have to clean his cell, but that was not much of a menial task. His cell was only seven-by-ten feet. It had in it a bed, a table and a chair. Some help was needed in the kitchen from time to time, and there was need for training in the liturgical parts of the chapel services.

But this does not mean that life in the monastery was easy. During the year of his novitiate, there were seven or eight hours appointed for daily prayer. During each of these hours the young monks who were not priests as yet were required to say 25 *Pater Nosters* with the *Ave Maria*. The priests had more detailed formulas to follow during those hours.

At this particular time in the history of the Erfurt monastery a new Vicar-General started making his regular visits to the monastery, namely, Johann Staupitz. He introduced a new code of statutes. One of these was an assiduous program of Bible-reading. He saw to it that every monk upon reception into the monastery received a Bible of his own. To make it distinctive, it was bound in red. Before long it was spoken of as the "Red Bible of the Augustinians." We know, of course, that Bible-reading was no new experience for Luther. He had been doing piece-meal reading of the Bible since his early school days. But now he did it so eagerly and learned it so devoutly that he knew large portions of his Red Bible by heart. This was, to be sure, St. Jerome's Latin text.

Staupitz, the new Vicar-General, soon took note of the melancholy young monk, Martin Luther. He treated him with fatherly confidence. He taught

Luther that for peace with God we must not look to our own resolutions to lead a better life, which we do not have the strength to carry out by ourselves. But we should patiently trust in the mercy of Christ and see in him the one whom God permitted to suffer for the sins of man — not as the threatening Judge, but rather as the loving Savior. Luther, both at that time and thoughout his life, spoke of Staupitz with grateful affection as his father and thanked God that Staupitz had helped him overcome his temptation to despair. Luther was sure that without Staupitz he would have perished.

Luther also was required to meditate upon the state of his soul, so that he might be in the correct state of mind to "confess aloud, discreetly and humbly," to the preceptor at least once each week. Once a week, at least, each brother had to enter the private confessional and reveal all of his sins, without exception. Luther did his best to unburden himself. But it was too much, even for a priest, to accomplish perfectly. There were occasions when Luther strove so hard to recall all of his sins that Staupitz would tell him "to go his way and come back another day when he really had some sins to confess."

We should not think, as we might be inclined to do in the case of a strong, healthy young man like Luther, that his constant efforts to confess resulted from sensual appetites. Luther does not seem to have been much troubled with that kind of weakness. His greatest struggle was with his inclination to become either angry or proud. Faults of that kind, in thought and word as well as in deed, were to his conscience deadly sins. To the priest who listened to his confession, however, they seemed too trifling to enumerate.

At the end of the novitiate Luther promised faithfully to live according to the rules of the holy father Augustine and to render obedience to Almighty God, the Virgin Mary and the prior of the monastery. Before doing so he put on a new gown which had been consecrated with holy water and incense. The prior received his vows, sprinkled holy water on him as he prostrated himself upon the ground in the form of a cross. When he arose his brethren congratulated him on being now like an innocent child fresh from baptism. He was then assigned a new and somewhat better cell, which looked out over the courtyard of the monastery. Unfortunately for researchers, that cell is no longer to be found. It was destroyed by fire in 1872.

What was required of Luther as a monk by way of ascetic practices was not excessive. He probably accustomed himself soon to eating only twice a day, and only once on each of the hundred-plus fast days. Perhaps his greatest discomfort lay in the fact that his cell was not heated. The rules of the Order forbade all decorations. The monk was not permitted to remove his attire, even at night, and he had to wear his little cap even within the cell. Any noise or conversation in the halls was strictly forbidden. To exercise, the brethren walked two-by-two up and down the cloister halls.

Luther's greatest hardships in the monastery were the hardships which he brought upon himself. His great unhappiness over his sins and his nagging sense of guilt drove him to think that if he were to torture himself, he might be able to drive evil out of his body. He was known to have fasted far beyond the requirements. One story is told so frequently that, although it lacks primary documentation, it is regarded as valid. It goes back to one evening when Staupitz missed Luther in the supper lineup. He had heard that Luther had been fasting excessively. This evening he decided to go to Luther's cell to investigate. Upon his arrival he found him lying prostrate on the cell floor, emaciated and half-conscious, with a knotted scourge lying beside him. It was one of the many occasions when Staupitz urged Luther to trust in the wounds of Christ rather than his own self-inflicted wounds.

There still was one other way in which Luther chastised himself, one might say, though he never would have considered it that. In addition to all of the other time-consuming practices mentioned above, he held himself to a right and lengthy schedule of reading and study, most of it in the Bible. It soon became known that his superiors had him in mind for the priesthood. Needless to say, he wished it for himself, if, for no other reason that this, that he might realize the joy which the "new baptism" of his monastic existence was supposed to have brought him.

For most of his second year in the monastery Martin devotedly prepared himself for the day when he might become a priest. He read the great words of Gabriel Biel, who followed Ockham in teaching that only Scripture revealed spiritual truth. He successively became a subdeacon, and then a deacon. After that he would become a priest. On May 2, 1507, the great day came. He was ordained and given the opportunity to celebrate his first mass. It was a day he would remember all the rest of his days, but not with pleasure. It did not bring him the peace and joy for which he longed. Overwhelmed by the sacredness of the moment when he was to offer up the blood of Christ as a sacrifice, he faltered. Had it not been for his assistant at the altar, he was sure that he would have run from the chancel. To falter in any of the many forms of the mass was considered to be sin!

One thing about that day did give him some satisfaction, though it, too, was not unmixed with regret. For the first time since he had entered the monastery, he saw his father, who rode into the monastery courtyard with 24 horsemen and a caravan of carriages carrying relatives and friends. His father came equipped to pay for the banquet, to which he had invited all of the participants and guests who were present at his son's first mass. Even his mother's uncle, Vicar Braun, attended, having been specially invited by Luther. At a proper point in the program Luther's father arose to speak. He scolded the personnel of the monastery, who were present in full numbers, for having admitted his son into their midst. He reminded them of the fact that the Scriptures include the Fourth Commandment. They should have reminded Martin of his duty to his father two years earlier. Luther was pleased to hear his father quote the Scriptures in such a gathering, but the message etched itself painfully into his memory.

Now that Luther had become a priest, his time became more his own. In other words, he had more time for Bible-study on an advanced level. And at this time, at the University of Erfurt, he began his teaching career.

During his last year at the monastery, Luther's state of mind grew more and more unbearable. All of his biographers speak at length about his spiritual struggle and ultimate breakthrough. They place an equally varied and lengthy list of interpretations on it and describe it with a variety of terms, such as the following: the monastic struggle, the period of the inner light, the inner conflict, *die Bekehrung* (the conversion), *die Katastrophe* (the catastrophe), *ein Turmerlebnis* (a tower experience), the quest, *ein Durchbruch* (a breakthrough), and the new theology.

In other words, as Luther approached the point where he could not endure his situation any longer, the stage was set for his emergence as the great Reformer of Christendom.

But how is it that Luther lingered so long and so miserably in his intense unhappiness, plagued by guilt and the fear of God's condemnation? We have to remember that Luther grew up in a church which taught a one-sided theology which interpreted virtually every passage of Scripture in terms of fear and punishment. Thus he grew up in a home given too much to thoughts about saint worship, the use of relics, salvation by works and the powers of witchcraft. Both state and church stood ready to defend the doctrines and demands of the papacy against the simple, comforting truths of the gospel.

When he first began to search the Scriptures earnestly, Luther relied on the "official" definition of terms like "grace," "righteousness," "faith," and "gospel" as they had been worked out by the scholastic theologians and philosophers. As a result he came to hate some of the Bible's finest statements. When the Psalmist prayed, "Deliver me in your righteousness," Luther shuddered. He hated the precious word "righteousness," because he thought it referred to a perfect righteousness which man was to produce in himself before he could be judged acceptable before God. He learned to fear, if not to hate, Christ. The thought that Christ would judge him in righteousness filled him with utter despair.

But there were other voices that would break through to rescue Luther. One was that of the great church-father Augustine. More than a thousand years separated their respective times, but Augustine had a message for Luther. It was not that Augustine could be followed in everything that he wrote, but he did write well concerning the sovereignty of God, the fall of man and the righteousness of Christ. Luther is quoted as saying that he was happy to discover that the ancient fathers had a clear understanding of God's grace in Christ.

Luther's most helpful voice, however, was the object of his increasingly diligent study, the Word of God itself. Though it is true that he did not fully grasp the meaning of the Word at once, yet he soon found himself in the workshop of the Holy Spirit.

During the summers of 1513-1515 Luther worked on his lectures for the fall terms, first on Psalms and then on Romans. Each time he came upon the expression the "righteousness in Christ" he paused to ponder and to examine the context in greater detail. Gradually, to his extreme joy, the meaning came through to him. The passage that unlocked the mystery for him was Romans 1:17. Suddenly he saw that the righteousness by which we are justified is not a righteousness which we must achieve, but the righteousness which Jesus accomplished for us on Calvary. That is the message of the gospel! And if the just are to live by faith, then righteousness, Christ's righteousness, is ours through faith; this, too, is a gift of God's grace, that is, of God's undeserved love.

Luther's *Turmerlebnis* was no bolt-of-lightning "conversion experience" on a given date, during a given hour, or in a given place. (The bolt of lightning, you will remember, moved him to cry out to St. Anne.) Rather, this was the Holy Spirit's blessing on the many hours his faithful servant Martin Luther had spent studying the Word.

Now Luther was ready to become an evangelical preacher and teacher. His sermons attracted many hearers. His lectures attracted large enrollments to the Wittenberg University. His was a new theology, indeed! Borrowing his terminology from the Apostle Paul, Luther spoke of it as "our gospel." It was new — as old as the promise in the Garden of Eden, of course, yet new. It was no longer the Antichrist's message of salvation by works. It was the gospel of God's mercy in Christ, of salvation through the "righteousness of Christ."

CHAPTER FOUR

THE REACTION TO NON-CATHOLIC OPPOSITION

If we were asked to list the most important facts about Luther and the Reformation, our first thoughts would probably include things like the 95 Theses, the Catechisms, the German Bible, the Leipzig Debate, the Diet of Worms, and documents like the Augsburg Confession and the Smalcald Articles. But the list should not stop there. There are a number of other documents and events which were of equal importance to the Reformation and the subsequent course of church history.

Martin Luther was barely beginning to see light at the end of the tunnel, so far as his reformation of the Catholic church was concerned, when he began to realize subtle and annoying opposition from non-Catholic sources. His dealings with the emerging Reformed theologies are as significant as his victories over Roman Catholicism.

Some twenty years ago, while driving through a sizeable city in central Iowa, I happened to round a corner on which there was located a Methodist church, undoubtedly the largest in that city. It was late October. Out on the yard in front of the church was a large, temporary billboard, which advertised the fact that this church would be celebrating the Reformation Festival. Not only were they going to hold several services with guest speakers, but in the evening they were also going to show the movie, *Martin Luther*, a 1950s-film produced by the former Synodical Conference. I had just shown it myself the previous week to the students in my Reformation course at Northwestern College.

As I drove on, thinking about the somewhat puzzling sight I had just seen, the thought occurred to me that they might indeed enjoy that film, since it pictured well the break with Rome but, agreeably for them, omitted entirely the important scene at Marburg. There Luther debated Huldreich Zwingli, one of the earliest forefathers of their church. Only eight years after the Diet of Worms, Luther needed to break fellowship with Zwingli, too.

Lutherans generally have a clear picture of the Lutheran Reformation where the Catholic Church is concerned, but are quite oblivious to the many significant differences between confessional Lutherans and other Protestants.

In his *History of Christianity*, Kenneth Scott Latourette writes, "Outstanding though he was as the great leader of the Reformation, Luther did not long carry all those with him who wished for change. Probably no one could have done so. So vital a movement inevitably had many expressions. Since they all had in common the repudiation of Rome, they were without an administrative head to enforce outward unity. Luther would not have done so even had he possessed the power. Before many years, numbers who at the outset were more or less sympathetic separated from him."

Likewise, Schwiebert, the author of *Martin Luther: His Life and Times*, writes "in the early stages of the Reformation Luther received an almost universal support in his challenge to Rome and its indulgence traffic; but as he matured as a reformer and his convictions crystallized, he began to encounter disagreement and opposition."

It was during the period referred to by these quotations that more and more non-Catholic voices began to arise in opposition to Luther.

The first such opposing voice technically spoke from within the Catholic Church, but his humanistic philosophy was in the process of alienating him from his roots. The man of whom we speak is, of course, Erasmus. Erasmus was not the founder of humanism, but at the time that he came into conflict with Luther he was known as the "Prince of Humanists."

Sixteenth-century humanism was the fruit of the intellectual movement which had spread north and west into the universities of the European mainland from the Italian Renaissance. Humanism fostered the study of the ancient Greek and Roman classics. It came as a relief to many who had grown bitterly weary of the old stereotype into which the scholastics had largely reduced Christianity by trying to reconcile the ancient Greek philosophy with Christian theology. The scholastics ("schoolmen," as they liked to be called), over a period of five centuries under the leadership of the University of Paris and the Dominicans, spun an intricate web of false doctrine from which the Catholic Church has not been able to extricate itself to this day.

Little wonder that when humanism came along with its rediscovery of the classics, men found it a relief. For one thing, they enjoyed the classics. Furthermore, the classics aided them linguistically in their exploration of the Scriptures. There was a short time when some of Luther's contemporaries spoke of him as a humanist. It is not hard to believe that for his love of the languages he would at first glance appear to be one of them. But his opposition to their philosophy soon became evident to them all.

For one thing, from the *Table Talk* we learn that Luther was much too busy during his early teaching days at Wittenberg and Erfurt to have become greatly involved with the movement as such. More than that, he quickly sensed that humanism was taking a wrong turn. While the exponents of the movement enjoyed reading about the adventures and accomplishments of ancient heroes, they soon became convinced that man is able to accomplish great things not only physically and socially, but also spiritually. When they placed their new-found notion alongside St. Paul's exhortations about sanctification, they arrived at the opinion that man could at least help to accomplish his own salvation, if not do it all on his own.

Luther did give the humanists fair hearing. He studied their works and addressed their issues. But when he found that a break was necessary for the truth's sake, he promptly and definitely took the step.

Erasmus first noticed Luther with the appearance of the *Ninety-five Theses* and immediately hailed him as a fellow-worker for the reform of the Roman Church. He regarded Luther as the champion of the gospel and the deliverer of Germany from the bondage of Rome.

At first, Luther counted on the support of Erasmus, and not without reason, for Erasmus spoke well of Luther's *Theses* and of the commentaries Luther had written in Wittenberg. In 1519 Luther addressed a letter to Erasmus speaking of him as "our glory and hope," acknowledged his indebtedness to him and even asked for his support.

It was not long after this letter, however, that we find Luther's enthusiasm for Erasmus cooling markedly. Luther wrote, "I am reading our Erasmus, and my opinion of him becomes daily worse. He pleases me, indeed, for boldly and learnedly convicting and condemning monks and priests of inveterate ignorance, but I fear he does not sufficiently advance the cause of Christ and God's grace."

And it was just in that area of God's grace in Christ that the basic difference between the two men turned into the need for separation. The clash reached a climax in the question of the freedom of will and predestination. The Prince of Humanists believed that man has the freedom of will to choose the morally good thing and to accomplish it, even in the area of achieving his own salvation. That thought led to another, namely, that God would be unjust and immoral if he were to order the universe in such a way that man could not himself fulfill the conditions which God ordained for salvation. He also asserted that God would be unjust if he arbitrarily chose some to be saved and by doing so condemned others to hell.

Erasmus argued that man's will must have the power to choose between good and evil, otherwise God would not have asked him in the Scriptures to choose the good. He further concluded that the fall of Adam had merely dulled man's moral faculties, but that man could rise above this, refrain from evil and choose those things which led to his salvation.

These were some of the thoughts which Erasmus expressed in *The Freedom of Will*, which he wrote in 1524. Many agreed that the book was a most remarkable document, clear, clever and tactfully written.

At the time Luther was preoccupied with the Peasants' Revolt and did not have an opportunity to reply. But one year later he did so in his book, *The Bondage of the Will.* In this book, Schwiebert tells us, Luther reached his peak as an able and well-balanced controversialist. Preserved Smith evaluated it as "one of the most important of all sixteenth-century works." Luther's reply was widely read. Seven Latin and two German editions were printed within a year. In later years Luther himself remarked that he would be willing to have all of his works perish except his *Small Catechism* and *The Bondage of the Will.*

In this book Luther takes Erasmus's contentions, one by one, and with a wealth of Scripture references sets each of his arguments aside. Frequently he turns to Romans 3 with its familiar passages like, "There is no one righteous, not even one; there is no one who understands, no one who seeks God"; 1 Corinthians 2:14, "The man without the Spirit does not accept the things that come from the Spirit of God, for they are foolishness to him, and he cannot understand them, because they are spiritually discerned." In this way Luther shows that natural man suffers the bondage of his will and does not have the freedom to choose that which is good in the eyes of God.

Luther goes on to show that salvation is by God's grace through faith in the Savior, and that it is the Holy Spirit who converts us and brings us to faith. It is true, then, that the new man takes over in us to lead a godly life. But just at this point Luther stresses two things — namely, that this is still not man's choosing but the Holy Spirit in us, and that even these deeds of the new man have nothing to do with salvation. They are his expression of thanksgiving to God and love for his Savior.

With respect to the heart of the gospel, Luther opposed Roman Catholic theology as well as the theology of Erasmus.

Erasmus never abandoned his position. At the same time he never really broke formally with the Catholic Church, though his views compelled him to wander unwelcomed from pillar to post. He taught at Paris, London, Louvain and Basel. He died at Basel in 1536 and was buried in a crypt in the Basel Cathedral. Nine years later, soon after the Council of Trent was convened, Erasmus was posthumously excommunicated and dubbed a heretic.

As Luther's influence was extending beyond the boundaries of Germany, another non-Catholic opponent appeared on the scene. Huldreich Zwingli had been born seven weeks after Luther on January 1, 1484, in a mountain village in the Toggenburg Valley of the Canton, or Province, of St. Gall in Switzerland. He was born into a locally prominent family. His father was the bailiff of the village. His uncle was a priest and later a dean, first at a school in Basel and then at a school in Bern. This uncle took Huldreich under his wing and convinced the young man to study under him at each of his schools. Zwingli was a brilliant lad. When the Dominicans learned about him, they tried to lure him into their monastery. His father and uncle became aware of their overtures and immediately transferred him out of harm's way to the University of Vienna. After his stay at Vienna he returned to the University of Basel, where he earned both his Bachelor's and Master's Degrees in short succession. While attending Basel he taught on the side at St. Martin's School.

Unlike Luther, Zwingli never became a Doctor of Theology, though this did not keep him by any means from his scholarly pursuits. He avidly studied Hebrew and Greek, mostly on his own, and devoured the works of Erasmus.

In 1506 Zwingli was ordained a priest and became the pastor of a country parish at Glarus. Here he worked for ten years. His stay gave him a good chance to continue his private study. While at Glarus, however, a double interest got Zwingli into trouble. He had kept up his interest in humanism ever since his university days. As a freeborn Swiss he also kept a close watch on political developments in the Swiss government, which was organized along the lines of a democracy. By Zwingli's time it also had become a tradition for Swiss soldiers to work as mercenaries for foreign rulers. The pope likewise maintained his papal states with the help of mercenary troops from Switzerland. Zwingli felt that the practice was demoralizing to the members of his parish. He knew what was involved, since during his Glarus ministry he had served as a chaplain for the Emperor's troops in the battle of Marignano. Before long, while still at Glarus, Zwingli began to speak out against the mercenary practice. As a result, he fell into disfavor with his superiors in the church and was transferred to a parish in Einsiedeln. Einsiedeln, which was not far from Glarus, was a center of attraction for pilgrims from Switzerland, France, Alsace and southern Germany. It was the site of a famous shrine which housed a black image of the Virgin Mary.

While at Einsiedeln he met a highly respected teacher by the name of Thomas Wyttenbach. Under Wyttenbach he studied St. Paul's Letter to the Romans and heard him say that only the Bible, and not the pope, is the supreme authority — also that Christ alone had paid the price for the remission of sins and that, therefore, indulgences were superfluous and that remission is unlocked to us by the key of faith and not by the keys of Peter or the church.

This is the message that was gaining popularity in Switzerland — Switzerland, couched in the hills to the south and southwest of Germany and the Netherlands, west of southern France and adjacent to the regions directly under papal domination. Antipapal feelings had been running high in Switzerland for nearly a century. The Swiss had refused to forget the local Councils of Constance and Basel, which were held in 1415 and 1432, respectively. These landmarks in papal unpopularity recorded the ouster of three popes, the unjust burning of John Hus, the near-ouster of Pope Eugene IV and failed attempts to bring about a moral reform of the church. The Swiss were not directly involved, but they were there, and they remembered.

We also recall that one of Erasmus's favorite haunts was Basel, a Protestant city in sympathy with Zwingli. These two men cemented their friendship by their mutual opposition, first of all, to Catholicism, and later, to Lutheranism.

During the turbulence which characterized the early and mid-1520s Luther was not able to give his undivided attention to Zwingli and the movement in Switzerland. Carlstadt's misbehavior; the raving of the Anabaptists, the Zwickau Prophets and the Mystics; and the culmination of disorder in the Peasants' Revolt, were enough to keep the Reformer occupied.

Zwingli's rise to prominence on Europe's theological scene began during his ministry as parish priest at the Great Muenster, the cathedral in Zuerich, the largest church in Switzerland. Although his first sermons there indicated that he was still Catholic in name, they did demonstrate that Zwingli was exceptionally able at explaining the Bible in a direct manner, free from scholastic explanations and legendary examples. And they showed his determined interest in uncovering ecclesiastical abuses. It was largely through his preaching that the selling of indulgences was prohibited in Zuerich.

In the meantime, Luther's attack against indulgences in Germany and his break with Rome was gaining sympathy for him in Switzerland. Many of Luther's writings were printed in Basel and sold throughout Switzerland.

And for a brief time during 1519 and into the early 1520s, Luther watched Zwingli with a measure of approval. As we have heard, Zwingli prohibited the sale of indulgences in Zuerich. He preached against fasting, private confession, the mass, monasticism, celibacy of the clergy, the use of pictures and music in the church services and the custom of fasting during Lent. In 1523 he suggested that all issues at stake should be clarified and settled at a formal disputation. In preparation for that disputation he prepared his *Sixty-seven Conclusions* in a format much like that of Luther's *Ninety-five Theses*. They agreed with Luther's theology with regard to indulgences, Christ as the only Savior and Mediator, the supremacy of the Word, rejection of the primacy of the pope, the mass, the invocation of saints, the merit of works, fasting, pilgrimages, celibacy, purgatory and on many other points. In fact, Zwingli once remarked that he was already preaching the gospel as early as 1512, before he had ever heard of Luther. But there is no corroboration of his claim.

Almost from the beginning, however, Luther was wary of Zwingli because of his radical views about pictures, music and ceremonies. Luther also disliked the mysticism and humanistic philosophy behind Zwingli's theology, as well as his excessive interest in politics. The subject which was to produce the break between them, however, was the doctrine of the Lord's Supper. Zwingli held to a figurative interpretation of the Lord's Supper. He taught that the Lord's Supper was only a commemorative ceremony in which the bread and wine only "represented" the body and blood of Christ. Luther and his followers believed that at the Lord's table we receive the true body and blood of Christ, since Jesus said, "This is my body.... This is my blood," and that through this sacrament we receive the assurance of the forgiveness of sins and the strengthening of our faith. There were several public disputations between the followers of the two opinions, beginning already in 1523. The first celebration of communion according to Zwingli's Reformed usage took place during Holy Week of April 1525 in the Great Muenster in Zuerich. By this time Zwingli's theology had developed far enough for us to be able to recognize him as the forerunner of the school of Protestant churches which we speak of as Reformed.

Philip, the ruler of Hesse, a German state on the route from Switzerland to the Netherlands, was a follower of Luther. Philip was greatly impressed by the fact that Zwingli embraced many of Luther's doctrines. He came to deplore the division which was becoming more and more noticeable and, as he saw it, disconcerting for the people of his principality. Therefore in 1529 he offered to sponsor a colloquy between the two leaders at his beautiful castle in Marburg.

By then Luther and the Wittenbergers already had come to the conclusion that it would be to no avail. Luther was convinced that Zwingli and his followers had displayed a spirit which would not bend. But much was being written on the matter, and enthusiastic followers of Zwingli were boasting that they would soon swallow up all of Luther's followers. Five princes, including the rulers of Saxony and Hesse, urged that a meeting be held. In fact, the Elector of

Saxony ordered the Wittenbergers to attend. The five princes now requested the drafting of articles on which to base their arguments with the Zwinglians.

Luther began work on these articles at once, He continued to work on them during the journey to Marburg and completed them behind the scenes during the colloquy. These articles, 15 in number, came to be known as the Marburg Articles, though their format and much of their contents resembled the 17 Schwabach Articles which Luther had drawn up for use among the German princes of northern Germany earlier that same year, 1529.

During the debate Luther declared that the clearest passage of all, was 1 Corinthians 10:16. If there were no other passages, this one would be sufficient, he said, to persuade all his opponents: "The cup of blessing which we bless, is it not the communion of the blood of Christ? The bread which we break, is it not the communion of the body of Christ?"

Zwingli's delegation arrived in Marburg on September 27. His principal companions were the theologians Oecolampadius and Bucer. The Wittenbergers arrived three days later. Chief among them were Luther, Melanchthon and Justas Jonas. Philip of Hesse welcomed the two groups to his Marburg Castle. Zwingli reported that 25 listeners gathered to winess the disputation. Another report estimated the audience at 50 to 60.

The debate at Marburg revolved largely around the Savior's words of institution. It is said that as the debate began Luther wrote the words of institution in chalk on the tabletop before him and then placed the cloth over them. From time to time he lifted the cloth to point out that the words meant just what they said and that they did not allow Zwingli's figurative interpretation.

For five days the debate went on. Since Prince Philip knew that Luther and Zwingli had a fiery temperament, he arranged to have Luther confront the even-tempered Oecolampadius and pitted Zwingli against the gentle Melanchthon. But when the five days were over, the meeting ended in an impasse. And yet, after the 15 articles which Luther had drawn up for the debate ran their course, disagreement seemed to remain regarding only one part of the 15th article, that which had to do with Christ's real presence in the sacrament. The two groups shook hands in friendship with one another as they parted, but not as a gesture of fellowship.

It is often reported that in parting with Zwingli Luther spoke the familiar words, "You have a different spirit from us." The record does not support that story, but it does report that Luther spoke those words to Bucer, the same man whom he refused to greet when arriving at Marburg. Luther just shook his finger at him and said, "You are a rogue." Bucer was a former friend who had come over to Luther's side in 1518 at the Augustinian Diet at Heidelberg. During the first years of the Reformation Bucer remained a loyal friend and supporter of Luther. But during the sacramentarian controversy he switched his allegiance to Zwingli. Thereafter he used his position as an editor to betray Bugenhagen on one occasion and Luther on another by giving the impression that they had written statements favorable to the sacramentarians. It seems, however, that on the day after the colloquy, in his retelling of the Marburg story, Luther left the impression that his words applied to Zwingli as well.

Zwingli's days were numbered. Two years later, in 1531, he fought in the battle of Cappel in a bloody war between the Protestant and Catholic cantons of Switzerland. He died there in battle at the age of 47. Fanatic foreign mercenaries among the enemies did not spare the bodies. Zwingli's body was quartered and then burned, and the ashes, mixed with the ashes of a pig, were cast to the wind.

Zwingli's theology was destined to find a new leader in John Calvin, the Frenchman who authored the famous *Institutes of Christianity*, which are accepted today as the basic confession of many Reformed churches.

True, there were some differences between Zwingli's and Calvin's theologies, but they were differences of form more than of substance. In time Calvin settled into the role of leadership in the church of Switzerland, a position which he filled from Geneva. And from that center his theology spread, under a variety of names, to France, the Netherlands, England and Scotland. From those countries it traveled in turn, to the New World.

The lives of Luther and Calvin did overlap for a short time, but the two of them never met face to face. In 1528, when Calvin was obliged to live in Strassbourg, both because of his exile from France and temporary opposition in Geneva, he and Luther did correspond by pamphlet. During their brief encounter Luther, it seems, admired Calvin for his brilliance, piety and integrity — three characteristics he had never been able to find in Zwingli. And while Calvin expressed regret that Luther often spoke too harshly, he was happy that Luther never came down heavily on him. As time passed, Luther was repelled by Calvin's legalism. But those were years when Luther was overwhelmed by a variety of grave responsibilities. His health often was not good. He simply let John Calvin go his way. He probably surmised that Calvin would do so anyway.

While speaking of Luther's dealings with non-Catholic opposition there is one more area that deserves our attention, namely, the movements which grew out of mysticism.

The mystics date back to fourteenth-century Holland and Germany. Their influence later spread into France, Switzerland and England. They were a group very much concerned about the reform of Christianity along medieval lines. They stressed pious living and closeness to God.

The chief of the mystics was Master Eckhart, who talked about an "inner light" and claimed to have had a direct experience with God. His disciple, John Tauler, was an earnest preacher and the founder of a group known as the "Friends of God." He also emphasized personal piety. Thomas à Kempis was the author of the *Imitation of Christ*, a popular work in which he urged Christians to live a Christ-like life based on the Sermon on the Mount. Another influential mystic was Gerard Groote, who devoted his life to reforming the clergy and teaching young boys. He is said to have been the founder of the "Brethren of the Common Life," a semi-monastic order of clergy and laymen which spread from Holland into Germany.

Luther studied under several men of their order in the cathedral school at Magdeburg. That contact with the mystics seems to have been harmless, perhaps even beneficial. Compared to coldness of the scholastics, the behavior of the early mystics was wholesome and heartwarming. They provided the young Luther with an example which may have influenced him later to inject sentiment and emotion into his hymns, his presentation of the gospel, and his frequent counseling.

Not many years passed, however, before the mystics suffered a change in personnel and attitude. With their emotional excesses and flippant approach to Scripture, they became a nuisance to the Reformation. Even Andreas Carlstadt, a co-worker of Luther on the faculty at Wittenberg, fell prey to this way of thinking during Luther's absence at the Wartburg in 1521-22. Carlstadt began to minimize the importance of theological scholarship and instead adopted the concept of "continuing revelation." He was hasty, radical and disruptive in his approach to reforms which should have been undertaken tactfully and in due time. Carlstadt was soon followed by Zwilling, an Augustinian monk who, with his emotionally charged preaching, became the leader of reckless bands of enthusiasts who literally vandalized the monasteries of Wittenberg.

About the time that these men were reaching the peak of their frenzy in 1522, they were joined by three visitors to the land of the Reformation, namely, the "Zwickau Prophets," who had traveled north from Zwickau on the border of Bohemia. These men — we know two of them by the names Stueber and Storch

77

— claimed that they had the gift of revelation and even ridiculed the value of the Scriptures. They said that if God had wanted man to use the Scriptures, he would have handed it down to them from heaven. While these voices were stirring up unrest and confusion, other voices predictably began to speak up against the social and political order. The peasants began to complain about their lot in life. They misunderstood Luther's emphasis on Christian freedom, by which he meant the freedom which the gospel gives us from ecclesiastical ordinances. To forestall complete havoc, Hans Mueller, one of the leaders among the peasants, drew up the "Twelve Articles." Most of these articles were reasonable. They claimed that the congregations should be allowed to call their own pastors, that certain taxes were oppressive and that the peasants should have the right to hunt and fish.

But soon another leader asserted himself among the peasants. He was Thomas Muentzer, an able and well educated member of the lower classes. Luther had earlier recommended him as pastor at Zwickau. But while there he embraced and began to promote the popular teachings about the "inner light" and "continuing revelation." He was a radical in every sense of the term. One Sunday, while Muentzer was preaching in Eisleben, the Elector of Saxony happened to be attending the service. Muentzer publicly denounced Luther and called out to the Elector to establish an apocalyptic kingdom. The Elector summoned Muentzer to Weimar for a hearing. But Muentzer fled from his jurisdiction and stoked the fires of rebellion which had flared up among the peasants throughout Germany. After having published several admonitions both to the nobles and the peasants, which for the most part went unheeded, Luther wrote his sharp exhortation to the princes to bring the peasants in line. It was entitled *Against the Murdering Hordes of the Peasants*. The peasants felt as though they had been betrayed. They began to speak of Dr. Luther as *Dr. Luegner*, Dr. Deceiver, and felt especially abandoned because of the pamphlet's untimely publication and distribution after the war was over.

The emperor's army was returning at that time from the Battle of Pavia, in which they had defeated the French. As they made their way back through central Germany, Elector John of Saxony, Landgrave Philip of Hesse and Duke Henry of Brunswick, whose states were much affected by the revolt, joined them to defeat Muentzer at Frankenhausen. Although Muentzer and Mueller were beheaded, the princes did exercise moderation in punishing the peasants.

We should mention one more item. Most of the mystics were Anabaptists, that is, they repudiated the baptism of children as unnecessary and ineffective and practised "rebaptism." It was largely because of that practice that the Anabaptist movement did not thrive, even though for a short time they were able to attract attention in Wittenberg through the Zwickau Prophets and in Zuerich through men like Hubmeier and Grebel. In their subsequent semi-oblivion, they made their dwindling way to other countries, even to the New World, under the name Mennonites, after the name of their later organizer, Menno Simons.

One of our goals in this chapter was to take a look at Luther's reaction to non-Catholic opposition. The other was to give enough of a description of the sources of that opposition to enable us to recognize their counterparts in our day. Humanism is still very much with us in its advanced stages. Professing that man is capable of choosing and achieving the good in all areas, modern humanism has absolutely no use for Luther's theology, and even considers it to be harmful to their goal of making this world a better place in which to live. The only gospel they will tolerate is a social gospel which glorifies man, his talents, his pleasures, his skills, his achievements and his possessions.

The followers of Zwingli and Calvin are also active today in the innumerable Reformed church bodies which appeal to reason as the final judge in spiritual matters.

Likewise, the mystics have their modern disciples in groups like the Pentecostals, who profess to be the agents of a continuing revelation.

Genuine Lutheranism, however, continues to build on the foundation of "Scripture Alone, Grace Alone, Faith Alone" — a foundation which is amply established and defended in the historic Lutheran Confessions.

CHAPTER FIVE

THE WITTENBERG PROFESSOR

When Johann von Staupitz in 1508 urged Martin Luther to accept a position on the faculty of the University of Wittenberg, little could he have realized the importance of his suggestion, not only for Luther, but also for the history of Christianity and the history of the western world.

Luther's teaching career, which spanned nearly 38 years, was spent primarily at the University of Wittenberg. This upstart school of higher education was the pride of its owner and founder, Prince Frederick the Wise, Elector of Saxony. As one of the electors, Frederick was one of the seven German princes powerful enough to participate in the election of the Emperor of the Holy Roman Empire. This was a distinct honor in a Germany which was made up of more than 300 independent states. Frederick took good care of his state and of his subjects, especially those who could be of benefit to him in turn. He loved knowledge and demonstrated a deep and sincere interest in religion.

Prince Frederick founded the University of Wittenberg in 1502. It had small beginnings, and the city of Wittenberg was itself a small city, with only about 3,000 inhabitants. But Elector Frederick seemed determined to change all this. He surrounded himself with able men who, in turn, selected talented and trustworthy teachers for the new university. Frederick entrusted the supervision of theology to Johann von Staupitz, whom he personally held in high esteem.

Staupitz was by no means an ordinary man. He had earned a Master's Degree in theology and had served as reader and prior of the monastery at Tuebingen, to this day a community of excellent reputation in scholarly matters. Thereafter he became a Bachelor of the Bible and mastered the *Sentences* of Peter Lombard well enough to be declared a *Sententiarius*, one qualified to teach that immense volume of Christian doctrine. To that he added his Doctor's Degree in theology and his licentiate, which gave him the privilege to teach theology. While serving as prior of the monastery in Munich, Staupitz was made Vicar-General of all the Augustinian Observantist monasteries in Germany. That gave him the responsibility of visitation also in the monastery at Erfurt where Luther received his training as a monk and a priest.

The Augustinian Order of monks was a conservative order, founded about a century after the Francisicans and Dominicans had been organized. It was founded as a protest against some of the deteriorating trends in the older orders. Among the Augustinians the Observantines were a group of conservative monks committed to "observing" all the rules.

Frederick the Wise wanted Staupitz to guide the development of his new University at Wittenberg. In our terminology he might be called the Dean or President of the University of Wittenberg. In 1508 Staupitz recommended Luther for a teaching post at Wittenberg. The fact that Luther was recommended by a man like Staupitz speaks volumes against those who try to portray the Reformer-in-the-making as being in any way unstable. Staupitz chose Luther because he had confidence in him.

Luther was not completely happy with his first assignment at Wittenberg, which was to teach Aristotle's *Ethics*. There was no doubt about his qualifications, but philosophy was not his favorite discipline. His interest in Bible-reading, already from the time that he was at the cathedral school in Magdeburg, led to a strong desire to teach theology. Staupitz undoubtedly noted that Luther spent all of his spare hours studying the Scriptures. In spring of 1509 the University granted him his Bachelor of the Bible. And now Staupitz saw to it that Luther would have his chance to teach theology. That explains why the fall of 1509 found Luther back at Erfurt. Here, for a period of two years, interrupted only by a four-month journey to Rome, he threw himself wholly into theology. He thoroughly studied the *Sentences* of Peter Lombard and earned the title of *Sententiarius*.

What made Peter Lombard's *Sentences* the object of careful study on the part of every medieval theologian? Peter Lombard was the man who during the twelfth century compiled in dialectic format a full list of the accepted doctrines of the church. In four long books he listed and treated them, taking his readers through a positive as well as a critical treatment of every doctrine of the Catholic Church. Lombard's work was the chief textbook of doctrine in the church until the Council of Trent in 1565.

Another matter of interest to us is Luther's trip to Rome. In the fall of Luther's second year of teaching at Erfurt Staupitz asked him to make the journey to Rome for the Order. This is further evidence of the confidence which Staupitz had in Luther. It so happened that there were Augustinian Observantine monasteries in Germany which favored a union with the headquarters at Rome. Staupitz, too, favored such a union. Luther opposed it. Staupitz sent Luther as one of two representatives to the Holy City to handle the matter. We know little about Luther's partner for the journey beyond his name and the impression that he was a man who favored the union. At first glance it appears that Staupitz sent one man of each opinion as a matter of fairness. Otto Scheel, in his detailed and dependable biography of Luther, suggests that since Luther was young and did not know his way around in Rome he was not expected to speak to the issue while there. It was a custom for monks and priests to travel in pairs on long journeys. Thus Scheel was of the opinion that the real leader of the two was Anton Kress, who came from Nuernberg. Perhaps Staupitz was hoping that Luther might come back convinced that he should support the union.

For Luther and the Reformation, this trip had considerable significance. It went a long way in helping to make Luther the reformer that he was. When he first undertook the assignment, he was enthusiastic about what a visit to holy Rome would mean to him by way of peace of mind and satisfaction with his lot as clergyman. His first shock befell him already when the two travelers reached Milan. Luther thought he would like to read a mass at Milan to express his thankfulness to the Lord for bringing them safely through the long and dangerous journey over the Alps. He found, however, that the Milanese were extremely proud of the fact that the great St. Ambrose had been their bishop at one time and that he had left them the Ambrosian chant. They told Luther to be on his way. "You cannot celebrate mass here. You are unable to perform the Ambrosian liturgy."

When the journey gave them their first glimpse of the Holy City, Luther felt the devotion of a pilgrim. All his life he had regarded Rome with awe and veneration. He fell upon the earth, raised his hands, and exclaimed, "Hail to you, holy Rome!" He later recalled how he had run, like a crazy saint on a pilgrimage, through all the churches and the catacombs. He wished that his parents already had died so that he could perform some special act to release them from the pains of purgatory.

But amid all of Rome's religious relics and treasures, Luther found no peace of mind. His soul was stirred to reflect on another way of salvation, the one which he had heard about from the Apostle Paul, namely, justification by faith. On his knees, in prayer, and with a papal promise of absolution, he climbed the sacred stairs which were said to have led to the judgment hall of Pilate. But on the way he paused for a moment as St. Paul's words suddenly interrupted his thoughts — "The just shall live by faith." Luther tells us, too, that he was shocked at the evident immorality of the clergy. He complained that the priests scrambled through their recitation of the mass as if they were doing a juggling act; while he was reading one mass, they finished reading seven. He was horrified at the way priests joked during the mass, and how they irreverently twisted the words. Someone standing close enough could hear them say, "Bread thou art and bread thou shalt remain." Still, Luther did express his happiness with the trip in later years. If he had not seen what he did in Rome, he said, he in later years and subsequent battles might have feared that he was doing the pope an injustice. But Luther did go to Rome. He could speak as one who was there.

The proposition with which Luther had been sent to Rome, namely, the union of the German Augustinians with the headquarters in Rome, failed. When Luther returned to Erfurt to resume his teaching, it seems that, although he and Staupitz still were friends, the strained feelings between the monks on the two sides in the union matter caused Luther to feel uncomfortable. For nostalgic reasons, he did not like the thought of leaving his beloved college town, but he was nevertheless relieved when, at the end of his second year of teaching there, Staupitz transferred him back to Wittenberg.

Here he lived and worked until the end of his life. He immersed himself in his tasks of lecturing, preaching, writing and counseling. From 1515 until the Diet of Worms in 1521 Luther served as the district vicar of the Augustinian Order. The only interruption during those 38 years was his memorable stay at the Wartburg, where he continued his writing and translated the New Testament into German.

Immediately upon his return from Erfurt to Wittenberg in the summer of 1511, Luther began to exercise all the rights and duties of a teacher of theology. He started with a series of lectures on the Psalms. When back in Wittenberg it again was Staupitz who influenced Luther's decisions. At first Luther had thought it would be best to leave Wittenberg and to devote himself to his office in the Augustinian Order. But Staupitz, as his superior, urged him to use his talents and abilities at the university. Elector Frederick, after having been deeply impressed by one of Luther's sermons, agreed wholeheartedly. There were times in later years, when surrounded by trials and dangers, that he regretted having given in to their prompting. Once he exclaimed, "If I had known then what I know now, not ten horses would have dragged me into it."

To assume his full professorship at Wittenberg, Luther was required to hold one more title and one more degree. The required title was that of licentiate. It amounted to a license which declared that he was qualified and obliged to teach the Bible at the university level. The ceremony at his induction included a solemn oath on Luther's part to defend with all his might the truth of the gospel and to preach the Bible faithfully and in its purity. This vow proved to be a great source of strength and comfort to him in the years to come.

There was a delay of several weeks before Luther was granted the final degree which he had earned, that of Doctor of Theology. The delay was caused by a lack of finances. But when Elector Frederick heard about the problem, he was prompt to offer Luther the required sum, which was considerable, so that his university could boast another doctor, and one at that who was already famous. The doctoral oath bound Luther to abstain from doctrines which were condemned by the church and offensive to pious ears. Obedience to the pope fortunately was not required at Wittenberg, as was the case at other universities at the time.

The story is often told of Luther's first reaction to Staupitz's urging that he become a doctor and a preacher. It happened while they were sitting under that familiar pear tree in the garden at the Black Cloister in Wittenberg. When Staupitz finished making his urgent plea, Luther at once cited no fewer than fifteen reasons why he did not consider himself fit to be a doctor. Upon Staupitz's further encouragements, Luther exclaimed, "Herr Staupitz, you will bring me to my death. I will never endure it for three months." To that Staupitz replied, "Don't you know that our Lord God has many great matters to attend to? For these he needs clever people to advise him. If you should die, you will be received into his council in heaven, for he, too, has need of some doctors." Luther acquiesced.

When speaking of Luther in his role as teacher at Wittenberg, we also have to mention his colleague, Philip Melanchthon. Melanchthon was a child prodigy who grew up under the influence of his great-uncle, Johann Reuchlin, the famous humanistic scholar in Hebrew and Greek literature. At age 13 Melanchthon entered Heidelberg University. His age posed no problem when he applied for his Bachelor's Degree. But when he applied for his Master's Degree at the age of 16, he was refused, not for academic reasons but because of his youthful appearance. He did receive that degree, however, at the renowned University of Tuebingen three years later.

It was Melanchthon's great-uncle, Reuchlin, who recommended him to the Elector of Saxony for a position on the faculty at Wittenberg University. He entered that faculty early in his 21st year. During his years at Wittenberg with Luther, the two men worked together in a firm bond of friendship and mutual admiration. Each complemented the other in a way that made of them an incomparable pair of teachers. James Richard, a biographer of Melanchthon, wrote, "Luther loved Melanchthon as a son, and yet often he sat at his feet as a pupil. Melanchthon learned his spiritual apprehension of divine truth from Luther. It is our impression that what Luther sought of Melanchthon was further training in Greek and Hebrew, and the theology which Melanchthon sought of Luther was in most cases practical theology."

In a recent article on the Reformation, Dr. Neelak Tjernagel commented, "In his public support of education, Luther had a skilled and effective associate in Philip Melanchthon whose leadership in education had earned him the title, 'Preceptor of Germany.' The author of many textbooks and the organizer of practical educational programs, Melanchthon had added much to the initial impetus of Martin Luther's sponsorship of education."

What kind of teacher was Martin Luther? His enthusiasm and consecration were undeniable. He was convinced that being a teacher was a precious calling, of all callings second only to that of the pastoral ministry, and even then second by very little. These are some of Luther's own words:

> I would briefly say that a diligent and pious school teacher or master or whoever the person is who faithfully trains and teaches boys can never be sufficiently rewarded and repaid with any money, as even the heathen Aristotle says. Yet this work is shamefully despised among us as if it were nothing whatever. Still we want to be Christians. If I myself could or should be obliged to leave the office of the ministry and other duties, I would rather have the office of schoolmaster or teacher of boys than any other office. For I know that next to the ministry this work is most useful, the greatest, the best. In fact, I do not know which of the two is the better, for it is hard to tame old dogs and to make old rascals pious. Yet this is the task at which the preacher must labor and often labor in vain. But one can bend and train young trees more easily even though some of them break in the process. My friend, let it be considered one of the greatest virtues on earth faithfully to train the children of other people. Very few people, in fact, practically none, do this for their own children.

Luther was a praying teacher. We read that he spent long hours in prayer. He was overheard and quoted on a number of occasions when he was praying aloud, though alone in his room. He continually discussed with his heavenly Father the problems which weighed heavily upon his heart. He asked the Lord to guide him so that he would give the best advice at all times to his students and to his parishioners.

Luther was a teacher eminently well trained for his work. He had a genuine love and a phenomenal capacity for learning and was at home with four languages: German, Latin, Greek and Hebrew. Even while lecturing extemporaneously (though he always prepared an outline for his lectures), he could switch freely from one language to another in order to clarify a point or to give an effective illustration.

Luther's learning was widely admired and appreciated, not only by his friends and students, but even by his opponents. Erasmus, the "Prince of Humanists," who is considered by some to have been the most learned man of his century, was once asked by Pope Adrian VI to address himself in opposition to Luther. Erasmus replied, "As to writing against Luther, I have not learned enough." James Froude, one of the greatest British historians, once said of Luther, "Luther's mind was literally worldwide; his eyes were forever observant of what was around him. At a time when science was scarcely out of its shell, Luther had observed nature with liveliest curiosity. He had anticipated the generative functions of flowers. Human nature he had studied like a dramatist. His memory was a museum of historical information, of anecdotes of great men, of old literature and song and proverb. Scarce a subject could be spoken of on which he had not thought and on which he had not something remarkable to say." Another historian called Luther the "Thomas Edison of his day." His contemporaries regarded him as a genius. Modern writers in our computerized age continue to say the same.

Melanchthon, the good friend and coworker of Luther, wrote, "Luther is too great, too wonderful, for me to depict in words. One is an interpreter; one, a logician; another an author, affluent and beautiful in speech; but Luther is all in all. Whatever he writes, whatever he utters, pierces to the soul, fixes itself like arrows in the heart. He is a miracle among men."

Luther was an inspiring teacher. His lectures were so inspiring that we are told that some of his students failed to take notes lest they miss a word. He was ready to admit that some of his earlier lectures were not as well done as he had wished, but that realization brought him back all the more promptly to his study in order to delve more deeply into the beloved Scriptures and to prepare all the better for his next lectures. Especially after he had come to a correct understanding of the gospel and of the righteousness of Christ, his evangelical lectures attracted more and more students from all over Germany, even from other European countries. Just as the famous Abelard once became the attraction at the University of Paris four centuries earlier, so that people said that Abelard "became" the University, so it was with Luther at Wittenberg. At the end of its first year in 1503, the enrollment at Wittenberg was 416, and it declined during the year following. But during the ten years after Luther came to Wittenberg in 1508, the enrollment increased steadily until it numbered over 1,000. Some 40 percent of these students came only to attend Luther's lectures. During that same time average enrollment was 100 at Leipzig University and only 50 at Erfurt.

Unlike many other university professors of the day, Luther drew many of his students into a bond of personal friendship. The slow student received helpful attention. He often went out of his way to find some merit in that which a slower student did have to offer, when he recognized honest effort on the student's part. He challenged the intelligent and advanced students. Yet he kept his presentation, for the most part, at the level of the average student. He was ready at all times to counsel his students, and he cautioned them against the temptations and vices of youth. The students freely sought his fatherly advice and counsel. He was their mentor both in the classroom and outside of it.

This is not to say that all the students necessarily liked Luther. He said himself that that would be too much for any teacher to expect. We have statements from Luther himself indicating that some of his students resented his efforts to accomplish a lot with them. Nor should we have the impression that his friendliness and concern for the students made him a soft touch. He was too clever for them. He could become very sharp at times. Knowing Luther as a man capable of frank speech, we can imagine that his discipline could be blistering. Luther hoped that in later years, when his students matured, they would still think back on it all in the right spirit and realize that he disciplined them for their own good.

At the same time, we find that Luther was a modest and humble teacher. He expressed his unhappiness with the students' custom of arising in respect whenever he entered the room. He said it would be better if custom were turned about so that the professor would bow to the class. Quoting one of his own teachers, he said that the professor could never know whether there might be a future mayor, doctor or lawyer in his classroom. His heart went out to the students who because of lowly background or poverty had difficulty staying in school. He was known on occasion to have helped some of them out with his own funds, even when it was a strain on Katy's budget.

As a teacher, Luther was indefatigable. Even during times of severe illness he carried a load that would have incapacitated the ordinary man in times of good health. His teaching schedule may appear to have been light at four lectures a week, one on each of four days, Monday, Tuesday, Thursday and Friday. But we have to remember that his preparation for those lectures during the early years of his career meant constantly researching and writing new material and working through the entire Scriptures, as well as the existing tomes of theology and church history. Then, too, he altered the courses he presented every year. Besides this, his 38 years of teaching were paired with a pulpit responsibility, first at the Black Cloister, then at the City Church and then for many years at the Castle Church of the Elector. This preaching schedule, especially during its latter years, called for as many as two and three sermons a day. Sometimes the festival seasons called for even more. And who of us has not marveled at the sheer volume of the collected writings of this man named Martin Luther?

Luther considered it his duty as a teacher to furnish all who followed him or studied under him an in-depth analysis and, where necessary, a refutation of the whole gamut of theories and trends which entered the stage during his long career — scholasticism, humanism, mysticism, the indulgence problem, the troublesome contentions of an Erasmus, the sharp attacks of a John Eck, the fickle opposition of a Henry VIII, the sacramentarianism of a Zwingli, the legalism of a Calvin, the misunderstanding of the peasants, the radicalism of the Zwickau Prophets, Zwilling, Carlstadt, the Anabaptists, and the like. Each of these represented a need to do fresh research, writing, traveling, and more preaching and teaching, to say nothing of long hours of counseling and consulting.

In closing, there is one surprising fact about this teacher, Martin Luther. Although teaching was close to his heart, he never put down in writing a formal list of directives which might be called a philosophy of education or methodology for teaching. One has to read widely in his works to gather his formal thoughts on the topic. But the excellence of his skill as a teacher quickly becomes evident to anyone who used his catechisms or ventures to read his lectures.

Of education, the Reformer wrote,

Let the teacher know his students as well as possible. Let him teach them as individuals for *their* good rather than to build up his own reputation or for the good of the school in which he serves.

One of the worst sins parents can commit where their children are concerned is not to give them proper education.

Where God's Word does not rule, do not send your child. All true education must be oriented with religion.

Education at the elementary level ought be universal. Young men beyond the elementary level who find higher education difficult or distasteful should be given vocational training, so that they might learn a trade and become valuable citizens.

Aside from a strong emphasis on religion and history, education owes another debt to parents and the state, namely to train the young, wherever possible, in music, the arts, and things cultural, so that they might use their talents and skills to the glory of God and for the good of their fellow man.

SELECT BIBLIOGRAPHY

Bainton, Roland H. *Here I Stand: A Life of Martin Luther*. New York: 1950.

Boehmer, Heinrich. *Der junge Luther*. Gotha: 1925.

Bornkamm, Heinrich. *Martin Luther in Mid-Career 1521-1530*. Trans. by E. Theodore Bachmann. Philadelphia: 1983.

Emme, Dietrich. *Martin Luther, Seine Jugend und Studienzeit*. Koeln: 1982.

Erikson, Erik H. *Young Man Luther*. New York: 1962.

Friedenthal, Richard. *Luther: His Life and Times*. Trans. by G. J. Nowell. New York: 1970.

Green, Lowell C. *How Melanchthon Helped Luther Discover the Gospel*. Fallbrook, California: 1980.

Grimm, Harold. *The Reformation Era*. New York: 1966.

Koestlin, Julius. *Luthers Leben*. Leipzig: 1882. Trans. *Life of Luther*. New York: 1927.

Latourette, Kenneth S. *A History of Christianity*. 2 vols. New York: 1953.

Lucas, Henry S. *The Renaissance and the Reformation*. New York: 1960.

Luther's Works (American Edition). St. Louis and Philadelphia: 1957-1986.

Manschreck, Clyde L. *Melanchthon, the Quiet Reformer*. New York: 1958.

Mathesius, Johann. *Dr. Martin Luthers Leben*. St. Louis: 1883.

McGiffert, Arthur. *Martin Luther, the Man and His Works*. New York: 1911.

New Cambridge Modern History (Reformation volume). Cambridge, England: 1965.

Painter, F. V. N. *Luther on Education*. St. Louis: 1889.

Plass, Ewald. *This Is Luther*. St. Louis: 1948.

Plass, Ewald. *What Luther Says*. St. Louis: 1959.

Richard, James. *Philip Melanchthon*. New York: 1974.

Schaff, Philip. *History of the Christian Church*. Volumes 7 and 8. Grand Rapids: 1950.

Scheel, Otto. *Martin Luther: Vom Katholizismus zur Reformation*. 2 vols. Tuebingen: 1916, 1917.

Schevill, Ferdinand. *The History of Europe*. New York: 1954.

Schwiebert, E. G. *Luther and His Times: The Reformation from a New Perspective*. St. Louis: 1950.

Siggins, Jan. *Luther and His Mother*. Philadelphia: 1981.

Smith, Preserved. *The Age of the Reformation*. New York: 1920.

Smith, Preserved. *The Life and Letters of Martin Luther*. New York: 1911.

Tjernagel, Neelak. *Henry VIII and the Lutherans*. St. Louis: 1965.

INDEX

Index

Luther, Martin,
 baptism, 6
 Bekehrung (conversion), 57
 birth, 5
 brother Jacob, 5
 discovery of Bible, 29
 Durchbruch (breakthrough), 57
 earned Bachelor's Degree, 37, 46
 earned Bachelor of the Bible Degree, 85
 earned Master's Degree, 38, 43, 44, 48
 earned Doctor of Theology Degree, 92
 education, on, 98
 family, 5
 first mass, 56
 inner conflict, 57
 Katastrophe (catastrophe), 57
 licentiate title, 89
 monastic struggle, 57
 new theology, 57
 ordained, 55
 parents, 7
 parents' discipline, 13
 period of inner light, 57
 praying, 93
 preacher, 96, 97
 quest, 57
 spelling of name, 6
 teacher, 94-96
 teacher's calling, on a, 92
 Turmerlebnis (tower experience), 57
 visit to Rome, 3, 86
 writings, 70
Lutheran Confessions, 80

Machiavelli, 2
MacKinnon, James, 10, 18
Magdeburg, 27
 cathedral school, 28, 29, 31, 43, 77, 85
 Mosshaus, 28

Mansfeld, 5, 9-12, 23-25, 31, 43, 44, 48
Marburg, 73
 Articles, 73
 Colloquy, 62, 72
Marignano, 69
Martin Luther (film), 62
Martin Luther: His Life and Times, 63
Mathesius, 8, 12, 15, 20, 27, 46
Matheson, 29
Medici family, 3
Melanchthon, 6, 8, 14, 17, 23, 26, 27, 29, 35, 40, 46, 73, 74, 90, 91, 94
Mennonites, 79
mercenary practice, 69
Methodist church, 61
Milan, 87
Moehra, 6, 9, 11, 16
Moenchsgewand (monk's attire), 51
monastic,
 attire, 51
 fratres (lay brothers), 50
 orders, 47
 patres (fathers), 50
Mueller, Hans, 78, 79
Muentzer, Thomas, 78, 79
mystics, 70, 77, 80
mysticism, 72, 76, 97

new baptism, 47, 51, 55
New World, 75, 79
Ninety-five Theses, 61, 64, 65, 71
Northwestern College, 62
Nuernberg, 86
Nullbrueder, 28, 29, 76

Observantine Eremites, 49
Ockham, William, 35, 36, 55
Oecolampadius, 73, 74
Oemler, Nicolaus, 23
Otto the Great, 4

Paris University, 63, 94
"Pater Noster," 52

Index

Valla, Laurentius, 4
via antiqua (old way), 35
via moderna (new way), 35
Vienna, University of, 68
Virgin Mary, 46, 54
von Paltz, 49

Wartburg Castle, 29, 30, 89
Weimar, 78
William of Anhalt, 28
witchcraft, 18, 19, 57
Wittenberg, 51, 65, 79, 83, 84, 90
  City Church, 96
    University of, 6, 10, 15, 24, 25,
      59, 64, 77, 85, 88, 89, 91, 94, 95

Wittenberg Edition (Luther's
  Works), 14
Witzel, 11
words of institution, 73
Wyttenbach, Thomas, 69

Ziegler, Margarethe, 14-16, 30
Zuerich, 70, 72, 79
Zwickau, 78
Zwickau Prophets, 70, 77, 79, 97
Zwilling, 77, 97
Zwingli, Hulreich, 62, 67, 68, 70,
  71, 74-76, 80, 97
Zwinglians, 73

104